Statistics to Success

4 Priorities Single Mothers Can Champion to Raise Successful Sons

Statistics to Success

4 Priorities Single Mothers Can Champion to Raise Successful Sons

Zachary Hawkins

Published by the Bodhi Collective
P.O. Box 323
Brookside, NJ 07926

With offices in
New Jersey Texas

Project Editor: JT Keitt
Cover Design: Pixel Prose Media

ISBN: 978-0-578-08303-2

Printed and bound in the United States of America
www.bodhicollective.org

Dedication

To mothers of boys everywhere, especially those who bear the responsibility alone; through you, we can witness the rebirth of a brighter tomorrow!

ZJ and Zion: new life, new legacy!

Acknowledgments

To my beautiful wife Karen, you have been my best friend, partner, cheerleader, teacher, and sounding board—I love you. To my sons Zachary and Zion, work hard and dream big. I know great things are in store for you—I love you both. To my daughter, Jazmine, my light when things seemed darkest—I love you.

To my mother, Joyce, thank you for hanging in there when things were tough. Without you, this story would not be possible. To my brother Jeffery thanks for playing such an important role in our lives while growing up and during the college years. You were certainly the voice of reason when it was needed; and to my little brother Tony, you have the biggest heart of anyone I know--you will forever be defined by it – I love you all.

To my wonderful extended family and friends too numerous to mention by name, thank you for your prayers and kind words over the years--I love you.

To my lifelong mentors, Carl Bisor, Raymond Holmes and James Patterson, you don't know what your presence in my life meant to me.

To my great friend Ray Cameron, we've come a long way since South Oak Cliff and Stop Six. Let's keep it going, because there is a lot more work to be done.

In memory of my Grandmother Thelma Hill, my Uncle Jerry Lawrence, and my father Jefferson 'Skipper' Hawkins, you will never be forgotten.

To the men of Alpha Phi Alpha Fraternity, Incorporated, HE chapter, you helped to smooth my rough edges and have provided a bond I can always count on. I am truly a better-made man because of our connection.

To Master Jae Hyeon Jo, I learned many valuable life lessons from you on my road to becoming a Black Belt leader. I am a stronger and more spiritually grounded individual as a result.

To all the single mothers I spoke with to sharpen my perspective—your courage inspires me.

To the many men I met over the years, especially my circle, (you know who you are), that share a similar upbringing whether through proximity or circumstance. Thank you for sharing your stories and giving me comfort in knowing that my past and destiny was not as unique and isolated as I thought growing up.

To all the young men I have met or have yet to meet that are not operating under the best of circumstances, I am issuing a challenge to you all to focus on what's possible. I want you to pledge to defy the statistics and reach for your piece of success!

Table of Contents

Foreword

When I first heard about *Statistics to Success,* I have to admit that I was a little skeptical. While I thought that it was definitely a worthwhile topic; I just didn't know what to expect. I thought, "Would he be sensitive to the struggles that, single mothers go through, whether we caused them or not?" After I read the book, I had two reactions; first, where was this book when I was raising my boys, and second, I can't believe I raised a son that could be this insightful and communicate his perspective in a way that honors and helps single mothers. We don't necessarily remember past events exactly the same way, but it did give us the opportunity to talk and get a better understanding of why things happened the way they did.

Single mothers have always had a number of negative statistics and stereotypes to deal with. I know it isn't the subject of this book, but I believe these stereotypes can add to the frustration we experience as we try to do the right thing for our boys. I know it probably will be next to impossible to change the thinking that seems to be "set in stone," but if mothers could take the opportunity this book presents, and place a real focus and energy on creating a new situation for all boys, people will have to begin to take notice.

I have been a mother for most of my life, and these statistics have always been troubling. However, just as I did, most mothers will continue to do the best they can for their sons, in spite of the numbers. I suppose, because people have access to information and news 24 hours a day, more focus is being put on the negative aspects of what is happening with single mothers and our children. I, like many women, certainly didn't set out with the intention of being a single mother—but there I was. When I embarked on the task of raising my sons alone, I knew it would be a difficult journey. It is my experience that many of us share the same concern of not knowing quite how to raise sons to become good men. If I had a dollar for every time someone told me "It takes a man to raise a man," I would be rich. I don't want to come across as though that is not a true statement; I just know that it really depends on the situation. It is certainly preferable to have a mother and father raising children but, it just depends. I am the proud mother of 3 sons. I had a lot of concerns when they were children, mostly financial. But I was also concerned that they were missing out on those things that everyone kept telling me their father could best give them—security within themselves and instruction on the things important for a man's development. In my opinion, the best part of what Zack has put together is a process and structure to exactly those things that, in the absence of his father, you should focus on with your own son.

Single mothers are some of the strongest people I know, and when I reflect on my role as a young single mother, what comes to mind most is my ability to make things happen when I really needed to; so hold on to that strength that is innate in us. When my boys were very young, my husband was in and out of trouble. But since I worked, we actually were able to provide a reasonable living for the boys and felt we could have a bright future. However, life came crashing down when my husband was sent to prison, with a 25 year sentence. Around the same time, my younger brother whom was also my best friend left home to attend college, and my father and I temporarily parted ways over very bitter circumstances. I was devastated and my body couldn't handle that much loss at one time. It is difficult to admit, but the impact these events had on my life were tremendous and I didn't handle that transition in my life well. I don't regret that I felt the way I did; my regret is that I allowed myself to be affected by it for so long. At that time, I certainly didn't model the type of behavior that I knew would be critical for growing boys—resilience. But over time, I fought the battle and was able to pick up the pieces. The reality is that I am not perfect, and you shouldn't feel as if you have to be either.

My advice to single mothers would be, to lighten up and don't beat yourself up for the decisions you have made or will make in the future. You cannot afford to neglect yourself, because you are all your children have. Also, make sure you treat yourself well, mentally and physically, and have a plan for your family so that everyone is moving in the same direction. Whether you are a single mother by choice or it was unplanned, I am here to say that with a little hard work, you can raise a successful son, whether his father chooses to be a part of the process or not. Another piece of advice that I would offer to single mothers is to listen. Listen to your sons as well as others who come offering sound advice. As a young mother, there were times when I failed to listen to and take good advice from others. I was immature, and stubborn about doing things my way. However, what I am most proud of is that because I was the mother of 3 boys with 3 very different personalities, I knew it would be important to parent them in a way that took those differences into consideration. Zack has always been open to other people's opinions and has welcomed involvement in new or different activities. I think this flexibility opened the door to other things in his life and as a result, he has been able to achieve a great life for him and his family. Reviewing this book reinforced how critical it is to do this. Boys without a father around can be a little resistant to new information. Zack offers numerous ways you can talk to your son and various tools to approach matters in a way that will encourage your son to accept the information.

In conclusion, I would highly recommend that you read *Statistics to Success* from cover to cover, if you are concerned about your son's long-term prospects for personal and professional success. When Zack started having children, I shared with him that the goal is for each generation to do better than the one before. I think as mothers we have to ensure that we do everything we can to break the cycle of negative statistics, so that the next generation of boys stands much taller than their fathers.

God Bless,

Joyce Hawkins

Introduction

I am blessed to have been raised by a single mother, and now that I have two sons of my own, I feel a strong desire to find a way to give back to a society that has offered me so much. While I don't profess to have all the answers or a psychological perspective, given the circumstances of my life and my desire to positively impact what is happening to young men in our society, I feel uniquely qualified to offer you this book. No matter what situation brought you to the role of 'single mother,' this book will provide a point of view from a man, several men in fact, raised by single mothers. I wanted to provide a perspective that focuses on the ups and downs you are going through as a family, and the challenges your son undoubtedly feels as he tries to understand himself and the dynamics of his life. Use the book as a resource to help fill the gaps that often make the difference between whether your son goes on to live a mediocre existence or one of unparalleled success. Even if you are married and your husband is not as involved as you would like, or absent for long periods of time, I believe this book provides a good point of reference and will support your efforts to make a positive impact on your son. Should I be addressing the failings of absent fathers? Absolutely, yes! However, this book was written to deal with the situation you face—today. You are the primary influencer in your son's life and are vital to what he is to become. I think we can accomplish something much bigger than trying to make adult men finally do the right thing. Together, we can turn these statistics around for our boys and stem the tide of another generation of absentee fathers.

"What exactly is my story," you may ask? While it is not completely unique; it is a story about beating the odds. As you read you may see glimpses of things you recall from your own childhood or people you know.

When my mother had her first child at age 16, the number of single-parent households was a bit lower than they are now. But even then, they carried a stigma with them. Three years later I came along, and when I was two my younger brother was born. My parents married shortly after I was born, but my father spent most of my childhood in prison. This reality seemed to be a vicious cycle for my family as my father was also raised by a single mother, his own father spending most of his life in the penal system. In fact, by sheer coincidence, he met his father for the first time while going through prison intake on his first major offense. My mother's parents were estranged as well. In this case, prison wasn't the culprit instead my mother's father chose the life of a 'hustler' over that of marriage and family.

We were raised on the south side of Dallas, Texas. Money was always in short supply. But thankfully, my grandmother, Thelma Lawrence, and my uncle Jerry Lawrence, were a constant source of financial and emotional support for us. During the very early years, life was actually uneventful. I was young, but can recall some good memories. It wasn't until my father was convicted for the second time, and received a 25-year sentence, that my mother's resolve was tested. The rigors of raising three boys alone were too much and beginning when I was about 9 years old, my mother suffered from debilitating depression and chronic illness. My brothers and I maintained a silent but fragile kind of security knowing that she loved us with everything she had and would keep fighting to ensure that in the end everything would work out well for all of us. Even in the midst of my mother's illnesses and the economic turmoil, my family always stressed education, and went to great lengths to ensure my brothers and I were presented with opportunities. As I understand things today, a couple of those opportunities, as well as an unplanned event, helped to shape the trajectory of the rest of my life.

You may already be aware of the statistics that surround single mothers and their children, particularly boys. I know them well because I used to be one of them. Statistically speaking, almost 60% of households are run by single mothers. I don't think that is such a shocking percentage, given that our divorce rate has crept above 50%. Furthermore, when you peel the layers back and look deeper into the statistics, you will find that significant problems within our communities exist and only seem to be getting worse. For instance, boys raised by single mothers are twice as likely to drop out of school. Given that the current dropout rate is above 40% for African-American and Hispanic children, this is staggering. Additionally, the same boys raised by single mothers are almost 40% more likely to spend some time in the criminal justice system and significantly more likely to use drugs, have discipline problems, and become economic underachievers. When I was young, those numbers weren't as bad, but they were still sobering, and in my community, statistics were trumpeted to us often. I was lucky. My mother didn't buy it. Whether by choice or by chance, she managed to carve out a life for my brothers and me that gave us a chance to not only beat those odds but in my case, far exceed the expectations society had for little boys like us.

As I look back over my journey, I have to smile because I can firmly attest to the old adage, "Life is not as much about how you start, but how you finish." Without any specialized skills or prestigious universities to my credit, I take pride in knowing that I managed to take my Bachelor's Degree, along with personal strengths honed over time, and turned them into something exceptional— a twenty-year career that propelled me from a mailroom in Dallas, TX to a key management role with a top firm on Wall Street. As I think about how my career has progressed, I marvel at how unlikely the experiences I have had would be for a kid growing up under the conditions I did. The bar of success for kids like me was low. 'Good' was often defined as simply staying out of trouble, staying out of jail, and staying alive to see another day. If you were able to make an honest living, you were really doing great things. As for my path, I called it unlikely a little earlier because no matter how accomplished I think I am, I have to give the credit for my success to divine intervention and a couple of well-placed life changing experiences. For that reason, I feel I have been called to share the lessons I've learned along my journey with young men who are experiencing circumstances similar to the ones I grew up under.

In the next section, Finding Life beyond the Statistics, I want to briefly share with you the life-events that made the difference for me, help you understand the origin of my point of view for the book, and encourage you to follow the steps and strategies I think you can champion to ensure a successful outcome for your son.

Finding a Life beyond the Statistics

As I mentioned earlier, I believe my life has been divinely blessed and I don't take that for granted. However, I am often asked the question, "Given some of the challenges you've faced earlier in life, what experiences helped to positively shape it?" Well, there were three very significant ones. I was able to immerse myself in something

I did well early, I was exposed to a world outside my own, and because of a life event that had an unintended consequence, I was forced to let go of the negative feelings I had for my father.

The drums were my passion. Growing up, I was always full of energy and to help me work off some of it my mother signed me up for drum lessons. I will share more about the experience later in this book, but to make a long story short; over time I showed a lot of promise, and learned how to channel my energy and quite frankly, redirect my frustration into something positive. Secondly, I had *exposure* to different things and people. In my youth, I spent many summers with my uncle and his friends, absorbing the college culture. As I became older, my involvement with Upward Bound, a government sponsored college preparatory program, helped to further shape my desire to attend college and make academics a priority. These experiences exposed me to a completely different group of people and a way of life to which I was not accustomed— one that would later benefit me greatly. It also helped me to understand the level of discipline that was needed to succeed in college. The third event that helped to transform my life was the unplanned arrival of my daughter. When I found out I was going to be a father, I was stunned. I was finishing up my final semester in college and had nothing but freedom and fun on my mind. However, once I understood the impact of what was happening, I realized that I had placed myself squarely into the same category where over 50% of boys raised in single-parent homes find themselves; being part of a new generation of single-parent homes—I was now responsible for perpetuating the statistic! It was a blow for me, but I was determined not to be the man my father was. First, I had to reconcile my thoughts about my own father. Understanding my feelings about him allowed me to let go of my anger and take the necessary steps to fully move into the next phase of my life. Getting married was not the right choice for me at the time, but being an important part of my child's life was. I immediately got a job, actually two jobs initially, and started the process of helping to support her financially and emotionally. While this part of my life was very sobering, I quickly realized it was exactly what I needed to ground me.

These experiences weren't particularly unique; however, what they did was open up my mind and heart to a life beyond the statistics. Those factors were also instrumental in my decision to move forward with this book. So, before I started writing, I wanted to make sure that it wasn't about "patting myself on the back," but a comprehensive piece that was, most of all, helpful to mothers and their sons. To make sure that I had a complete perspective, I pulled elements from my own experiences growing up, and over the years have met, made life-long friends with, and talked at length with many men that had a childhood similar to mine. Some have achieved great personal and professional success, but for various reasons, many have not. However, in this book I attempt to capture and bring forth the collective understanding of all those experiences.

Throughout this book, I will refer to a group of these men that I keep in touch with on a regular basis as my "circle." Single mothers raised many of them. This book has a heavy influence on the ABC's of raising boys, but more importantly, it shares strategies you can employ to help your son achieve his full potential and ultimate success. The strategies that I propose have been adopted over the years in one form or another by all of us. Using many of these strategies, most of the men in my circle have achieved a high level of personal and professional success. During my 20 to 30 years of talking, sharing, and 'strategizing' with these men, I've heard a lot of positive and triumphant stories about their determined and hardworking mothers. For those that were raised by a single mother, I recall that our discussions would become more restrained as the conversations evolved to include more emotional accounts of the journey with their mothers. In my view, the reason for their restraint in discussing the emotional or potentially negative reflections is because most men, whether they admit it or not, feel it is a bit taboo to talk about mothers, especially single mothers, in less than glowing terms. Perhaps this is because, at the very least, their mother was the parent who was around. All of these men were clearly appreciative of the work their mother put into rearing them and couldn't imagine life without her. However, the goal of this book is to attempt to address the full range of feelings and turning points that your sons experience in your journey together as a family (good and bad).

When I shared with my circle that I used the essence of the conversations they shared with me over the years as background information, they were excited to provide further clarity, read final chapters, etc. They all felt an obligation to help single mothers, especially if the ultimate benefactor would be her son. Most of the men in my circle used many words to describe the relationship they have with their mothers, as well as their assessment of her role as primary caregiver and household manager. "Loving, dedicated, wise, cash-strapped, disorganized, sad, and angry," were the traits most often referred to and when speaking about themselves, the words "appreciative and conflicted" came to mind. I echo those words too, because I had a deep appreciation for my mother; she took responsibility for us and did what she could to keep it all together, but I also felt conflicted because of the more critical feelings I had about how she managed some aspects of that responsibility. In retrospect, we all realized that many of the things we felt we missed growing up, our mothers had within her to give. But what often got in the way of our families being more prepared, or our mother's ability to make decisions that weren't so emotionally charged, was most likely, the lack of a clear long-term plan, and the habit of operating almost on auto-pilot from one stress to the next. We realize now, that mothers in general tend to overlook their own needs, moving forward at times as if she is indestructible. Whatever the reasoning, she rarely took the time or the steps needed to properly manage the constant stress in her life. Unfortunately, the combination of feeling as though we were oftentimes lacking in direction and had mother's that were often stressed to the max, left some of us uncertain if we could successfully handle the bigger challenges of life.

Later in this section I will introduce a set of 4 Priorities you can incorporate as you work toward developing that clear plan (long and short-term) for your family. As for how you should go about managing the stress; once you get through the priorities, if you feel you still need more strategies to help yourself get through the day-to-day, take a look at some quick tips I've included at the conclusion of this book, I think you will find them helpful!

In trying to blend all the different perspectives, I also spoke with single mothers, just like you, representing every color, income level, religion and perspective, to understand the concerns you have about raising sons. A common thread that seemed to resonate among these women was that what hindered them, seemed to be the lack of time or financial resources, or the lack of knowledge required to raise a successful son. What also resonated were the understandable insecurities single mothers have about the inability to relate to what their sons are going through at critical points in his life. Finally, in my research, I compiled and reviewed relevant information and resources to support you and your efforts to raise great boys. I found numerous books and websites on the subject (all have been included in Chapter 9, Leverage Mentors, Role Models and 100+ Resources). Mental health professionals have written most of the information and advice available. These professionals seemed to focus a great deal on the psychology of boys—which is helpful. I found other books written by women with firsthand experience, which revealed a camaraderie that I can imagine is irreplaceable. However, there wasn't much material available from a male perspective, and even fewer resources available that took all of the points of view provided within this book into consideration. I think any book on the topic of parenting is of value, however, I wrote *Statistics to Success* to serve as a parenting roadmap, addressing the intricacies of the unique relationship between single mothers and their sons, and the types of things you should focus on to champion his future success. I don't use the term 'champion,' lightly. But like no other; when mothers have the right tools they can mentor, motivate and help her children manage the most challenging aspects of life. I would consider that a true champion for her child—right?

First, I want to say that this book was NOT designed to place the responsibility of your son's development, or in some cases "change in direction," all on you. Ultimately, it is up to your son. So, how should you get the ball rolling? Before I answer this question, I want to preface it by saying that all mothers, especially single mothers, are definitely underappreciated for the phenomenal job you do. However, even the most skilled professionals have to stop every now and again and take an inventory of how well they are performing their duties. With the goal of sharpening skills, I ask, "How are you handling your role today as primary provider, mother, role model, mentor, and motivator? Please be honest with yourself. Are you angry, stressed or distracted? I understand all of that, and you know—it's actually okay. Second, I want to reiterate that to get the ball rolling may require you to make a couple of changes in your own life in order to be the example your son needs. "Do as I say, not as I do," didn't work for our generation and it won't work for your son's. Third, with purpose in your mind and heart, be determined to consistently follow the set of 4 parenting priorities identified in this book. You can use the priorities as a guide to help your son achieve tremendous success against the odds.

When I was in the research phase of developing the content for this book, some mothers I spoke with suggested that she was already doing what was being proposed in this book. Well, let's take a close look at that suggestion. Truthfully, most parents (single parents and two-parent homes) don't look at raising their children strategically, and we are certainly very inconsistent with the messages and behaviors that we model—I know I was. But given our fast paced society and the day-to-day pressures of life it is easy to get sidetracked. Unfortunately, collectively we have allowed the bar to slip for our children and for ourselves. We've traded in greatness for good enough. So before our good-enough expectations slip even further, I am suggesting that we challenge ourselves to move the bar back to greatness—starting with our boys and I believe you, as mothers, are in the best position to make this happen.

Are you willing to take on the challenge? Are you ready to usher in a new era of thinking and living, for you and your son?

Based on my experience, as well as the strategies discussed over the years with my "circle" of friends, I developed a set of <u>4 Priorities</u> that were most critical to our development and ultimate path to achieving success. For the men who were raised with strong fathers in the home, they seemed to have been introduced to these priorities in their normal development within the family and had only to refine them as they matured. For the rest of us, we used a myriad of things to compensate for not being exposed to a more methodical and comprehensive approach to managing life early on: mentors, happenstance, luck, grace, etc. we don't take any of these things lightly because without them, our lives would have probably turned out differently. Additionally, it is not to say that by placing these 4 priorities in your parenting 'bag of tricks,' your son won't encounter difficulty—he will. The goal is to help him start the journey with a roadmap and hopefully fewer unnecessary burdens. The 4 Priorities I am setting forth are as follows: *Priority 1, Establish Healthy Relationships; Priority 2, Achieve Self-Mastery for Strong Character; Priority 3, Pursue Every Opportunity Proactivvely; and Priority 4, Envision a Path to Success.* The Priorities are defined in Figure 1, in greater detail.

Throughout the course of this book, I will identify how you can help your son grow and develop, using these priorities in greater detail. Within each priority there are 3 areas of focus along with corresponding strategies that suggest how you can help impart the information to your son or develop the characteristics within him. The priorities are structured to provide better clarity however, each priority can stand alone, or be taken and highlighted as you deem most appropriate for the situation.

	Establish Healthy Relationships
Priority 1	Helping your son establish the right kind of relationships with others, including his father will hinge on the type of relationship he has with you.

	Achieve 'Self' Mastery for Strong Character
Priority 2	When your son masters the critical areas of Self-Discipline, Self-Respect and Self-Direction, it will give him the fortitude to succeed in all areas of his life.

	Proactively Pursue Every Opportunity
Priority 3	When you make the most of your son's educational experience, encourage a disciplined attitude toward money, and take advantage of available resources; your intiative will make a difference.

	Envision a Path to Success
Priority 4	Help your son define a path to success. Using his natural talents as the basis, guide your son through the process of developing a plan for his future and highlight what he must do to make the plan happen.

Figure 1: 4 Priorities Single Mothers Must Champion

Priority 1
Establish Healthy Relationships

"The most important single ingredient in the formula of success is, knowing how to get along with people."

Theodore Roosevelt

The fullness of our life is often determined by the quality of the relationships we possess. Our primary and most important relationship is the one we establish with our parents. The better and more balanced the relationship, the more confident and well adjusted the child will be. Because of this, it is so very important that a positive, balanced relationship is established with your son. You should also support and encourage his need to explore what type of relationship he can have with his father as well as the various types of relationships he can have with others. Through the experiences and interactions he witnesses between the adults in his life, he will establish his approach for how he manages these relationships. All of your son's relationships won't be positive, so encourage him to accept and learn from all types of relationships—good and bad. Boys, especially, should be exposed to the full range of emotions that relationships provide and be taught how to manage them. This skill will give your son the inner strength required to stick with intimate relationships long-term, and the tools to deal effectively in most professional settings. Because if you didn't already know this, the 'politics,' most people refer to in a corporate sense really boils down to basic relationship management. The better he is at this, the greater chance he will have of navigating successfully through tricky professional waters.

In *Priority 1*, three key factors are critical in helping your son establish healthy relationships. *First, understand why you should approach your relationship with your son as a partnership; second, learn how to avoid creating dynamics that could negatively influence your son's behavior and diminish his ability to have long lasting personal and professional success; and third, by giving him guidance and support, encourage your son's effort to establish healthy relationships with others including one with his father.*

I can vividly recall the types of interactions my mother would have. They typically fell into two categories: Type one was when she interacted with family and friends—it was very easy-going and there wasn't much need for formality or negotiation; the second type of interaction was when she had to deal with things like government bureaucracy or collectors—it was typically a much more tenuous dialogue. Unfortunately, this stark contrast offered very little in helping me understand how personal and professional relationships really work. As you know, most boys already find managing emotions and relationships a little tough. When we are given limited opportunities to acquire the skill set to understand and manage relationships, it makes it even more difficult. While it may seem obvious that you should teach your son how to communicate, establishing and maintaining relationships is quite a different matter. I am sure you've heard countless stories about people who take the wrong path in life—most if not all were surrounded by unhealthy relationships. So be sure that this priority isn't taken lightly. If you give him the tools and knowledge for cultivating healthy relationships, it is unlikely that he will be influenced by negative peer pressure or engage in inappropriate behavior.

Chapter 1

Create a Partnership with Your Son

Highlights	
"Single mothers should establish a partnership with their sons, not one of equals, but one of responsibility."	
– Managing Projects Cultivates Self- Motivation – Finding His Own Voice	– Stepping Outside of His Comfort Zone – Learning to Handle Consequences

Hopefully you already have an inter-dependent relationship with your son, where he is growing in his independence but still relies on you for support and guidance. If so, you have already established the basis for the type of relationship I think you should create with your son—a partnership. *I am not suggesting a partnership of equals, but a partnership of responsibility.*

Running a family is a lot like running a small business. So I would encourage you to think of yourself as the 'Managing Partner.' In that role, you are tasked with getting the rest of the team engaged and on board with your direction and the family's collective vision. Everyone on the team has responsibilities, but in order to be effective, everyone must feel as though they have a stake in the success or failure of the family business. You achieve this by giving everyone a voice and a role in the process. The partnership I am suggesting will help you achieve that. Therefore the first thing you must do is establish parameters around this partnership.

As parents, I believe we all should love our children unconditionally and provide them with the necessities of life.

Increasingly, I believe that one of those necessities is to be diligent about getting them on the right track and coaching them through the 'finish line.' This is a tough assignment because, let's face it—it is a job that takes twenty-plus years. With that much time, it is very easy to get sidetracked. Having strategies that the two of you can reflect on or refer to along the way will keep you and your son honest about what is needed to ensure his success. It will also better prepare you for the eventual reality that your son will be moving on to start a life of his own. In this partnership your duties will change from time to time. Yes, you are his mother, but you are also his provider, motivational coach, mentor and role model, and therefore, you need to analyze each situation first to determine what role is required, and be steadfast in your resolve to assume that role based on the situation. Here are a few strategies to help you manage this partnership and keep those revolving duties in line. You can help him manage the monotony of life and rigors of his growth and development, one project at a time, by *Managing Projects for Self-Motivation, Helping Him Find His Own Voice* through shared and independent experiences, *Encouraging Him to Step Outside His Comfort Zone* and *Helping Him Learn to Handle the Consequences* of his decisions whether the result is bad or good.

Managing Projects Cultivates Self-Motivation

Project management is a very adult term, however I find it can be very useful for boys too. When there are a series of projects or goals your son can work on and manage to completion, it helps him learn to advance his life one step at a time or in this case, one short-term project at a time. This will keep your son busy and help him manage the monotony of life--gaining confidence and skills with each project he completes.

During these projects, your responsibility is that of 'coach' and primary 'motivator,' so you should work with him to identify each project or goal he wants to pursue and motivate him throughout the process. With most everything, consistency is the key. Your son will be responsible for sticking with his project and you will help by consistently motivating him through the finish line. I find that children, boys in particular can sometimes lack self-motivation. It is up to us to help instill the desire in them. Becoming self-motivated happens at different times based on the individual, but should happen as a young man matures. However, engaging him in these types of project-based activities will help him to become self-motivated sooner. As he grows and has a history of successfully completed projects under his belt you will find that your role as motivator will diminish.

The purpose or type of project/goal can be whatever your son chooses; academics, extra-curricular activities, etc. When helping him decide, keep in mind that projects are naturally more tangible, like putting together a model airplane; while goals are intangible, for example, improving his time in a race. Whether your son prefers projects, goals, or a combination of the two, I would suggest that you find things that keep his interest. Consider these ideas for identifying and keeping track of each project:

1)   Be Consistent – On a regular basis, sit down and help him identify what he wants to achieve, whether it is to improve his grades for a marking period, or win his first 100-yard dash.

2)   Establish a Plan – To ensure a successful project, he should establish a plan with specific steps and milestones to be completed and write it down. In the process of identifying what steps he needs to take, make sure his plan is measureable and he has a timeline. Below is a very simplistic example, to hopefully remind him that there is nothing complicated about this:

Goal: Improve 100 meter time
- Achieve by the second track meet
- Improve my time from 14.00 to 13.50
- To accomplish this goal, I will work out for 1 extra hr each day

3)   Check Progress – Encourage him along the way by checking his progress, and help him tweak the plan if needed. Even if he attends practice faithfully and works really hard, his times may not improve because he has been eating ice cream at lunch every day. Well, it is very possible that the ice cream may be the problem. As his coach, identify what might be hindering him from achieving his goal and encourage him to change his behavior, or make adjustments to the goal if needed.

4)   Evaluate Results – At the end of the project, evaluate and relish his achievements with some type of acknowledgement (telling him, "how proud you are," is typically enough). Remember

achievements are relative. Did he accomplish what he set out to do? Did he stay on task? Maybe he didn't meet his goal, but he did show improvement. When the project ends, discuss where things may have fallen short and help him determine what could be done differently next time.

Finding His Own Voice

These days, serious dialogue with your son has to begin at an earlier age because we are bombarded with information from all directions, and with that free flow of media you never know what he may hear or see. Therefore, establishing an effective way of relating to and communicating with your son is important, as it will also help him better understand what he thinks and feels about what he is hearing. When your son begins to manage this information along with thoughts from you, friends, other family members, and teachers, he could become overwhelmed if he doesn't feel comfortable invoking how he thinks too. His level of confidence will rest heavily on his ability to find his own voice and articulate what he thinks and feels at all times.

Both men and boys need space to think about our feelings. We are much better at coming back to a topic after giving it thought to express our feelings about a particular subject. This has been most apparent to me with my own sons. I've learned that the best way to get them to open up is when we are doing something unrelated to the topic. For example, if I want to know what's going on at school, I can find out more information while tossing the football around on the playground. If you push your son too hard and require information immediately, he will more than likely shut down. If this has been difficult for you, I would recommend doing something like I just described in the example above. You could also consider touching on the topic, tell your son to think about it, and find an appropriate time to come back to it. Boys, especially those who don't have a father around, have a lot going on emotionally, and they are trying to make sense of it. He may not know how to convey his thoughts and feelings early on, but that will come with time.

In your quest to get him talking, make sure that he is also thinking. Ask him open-ended questions or require that he respond in complete sentences. When he does open up, at times you may feel compelled to question the validity of his feelings, DON'T. Remember boys are hardwired differently. However as he gets older, the decision not to question his feelings will go a long way in establishing a partnership built on trust—trust in you and trust that you will always listen to him without judging him. Also, if verbal communication is difficult for him, encourage him to express himself by writing his thoughts down on paper. I cannot over-emphasize the importance of getting him talking and thinking so that he can find his own voice. I firmly believe that if you make mistakes in other areas of his development, good communication, especially on his part, can help you recover more easily.

Stepping Outside of His Comfort Zone

Being exposed to new things was one of the best things that happened to me. Including this as part of your partnership is a good way to help your son gain confidence and learn to assert his independence. In my personal and professional life, I have taken on roles and done things that were completely out of my comfort zone. I left the comfort and familiarity of Dallas, Texas, and moved my young family to the Northeast where we had no network upon which to depend. Now after 10 years, we are thriving and enjoying a very different and more fulfilling way of life. When we announced our plan to move, I recall how many of my friends and family thought that going so far away was an extremely risky proposition. I knew they were right, but I kept my eye on what the result would be if things went well. I believe the courage to do these kinds of things came as a result of my early years. When I was around 10 years old, I began drumming competitively and was placed in increasingly uncomfortable situations, sometimes alone as my mother was not always able to come to my events. I was fortunate that I was able to make the connection from my early years, to my professional and personal life, because it certainly has come in handy.

To get your son outside of his comfort zone, I would recommend that you place your son in situations that challenge him. For example, if your son is shy, encourage him to shake hands with people as he meets them, (this is actually something good to do even if he isn't shy). As he gets more comfortable, have him go into a store and ask for directions or another appropriate question. As he gets older, have him join activities or competitions he may not have tried unless you encouraged or in some cases, insisted on it. As you can see, the point is to gradually help him feel comfortable trying new things, increasing the complexity each time. If your son is not naturally curious, it will help him move out of his comfort zone, and he is more likely to be prepared when he is thrown into new situations.

Learning to Handle Consequences

Dealing with disappointments, or the negative consequences of your actions, can be a difficult time in a young man's life regardless of his age. How he handles the disappointment will be a critical life lesson for him as a man. While the goal of this book is to help minimize some of the unnecessary burdens that can fall upon your son, no amount of preparation, support, mentoring, or protection can completely shield him from adversity. Any man who has achieved a measure of success has had his fair share of setbacks. Successful men are able to rebound quickly from a setback and move forward with determined purpose. Just as diamonds are formed under pressure— challenges are necessary, so that we can become who we are truly meant to be. Give him the space to put the pieces of the puzzle together on his own and he will gain more confidence with each step.

Just when you think that he has it all together—SLAM, he falls on his face. At this moment, he needs someone to empathize with him, give him a few pointers, then tell him to dust himself off and get back out there again. In defining the parameters of your partnership with your son, this is the point where you take on the responsibility of mentor, providing support and wisdom to your son. In times of trouble, a good mentor will encourage you while pointing out the lessons that can be learned from the situation. Highlight what actions or behaviors he should consider changing next time. Your son will find comfort in this and go forward with the confidence that, at the very least, you believe he can conquer the challenges before him. It is when men face disappointments that we are most vulnerable and as men we need to feel there is a safe place to go and regroup.

With that being said, you have to resist the temptation, albeit painful, to rescue your son. This is obviously based on age appropriateness and the situation because, as a parent, there are times when intervention is needed (but as he grows, it should be with less frequency). If you make a habit of rescuing him, STOP or it will do harm to the man he is to become.

. . . .

If this is going to work as an effective partnership, you both must play a role in establishing the parameters as well as getting the work done. Remember, if he is at the table, he will be more willing to take ownership of what you decide together and be more likely to fulfill his part of the deal. When you have his buy-in you will have a greater chance of making *Priority 1,* a success. By forging a partnership with your son, you will move closer to helping him realize his true potential and more importantly, establish a healthy relationship you both can enjoy.

Chapter 2

Know What Type of Man Your Relationship is Creating

Highlights	
"When you don't have the balance of a father in the home, I believe unknowingly, the mother/son dynamic can sometimes result in negative personality traits in her son."	
– The Underachiever – The Drill Sergeant	– Momma's Boy – Henpecked Man

Mothers share a special bond with their sons regardless of the circumstances. A mother's love has the ability to make her son stronger, and help provide balance in his life by helping him think from his heart. On the other hand, a father's love provides security and strength of character, which helps the son feel that he is able to take on the world. If your son's father is not around, you are tasked with helping him develop in all of these areas. Given the right circumstances, some mothers can pull this off. However, when you don't have the balance of a father in the home, I believe that unknowingly, more and more often, the mother and son relationship could be resulting in the creation of men that take on one of these 'negative' personalities: The Underachiever, Drill Sergeant, Momma's Boy, or a Henpecked Man.

Over the last 40 years I've spent a lot of time with men that have a mix of these personalities and I believe these types of men are a big part of the reason why we have so many failed marriages, so many children who aren't being taken care of, and some really good women who more than likely will never be taken care of. While these men are not being exclusively raised by Single Mothers, in my experience you represent a large majority of the parents that raise them. While I agree that a father's absence is probably the genesis of this problem; however, it is the way you choose to manage the relationship between you and your son that will play an even bigger role in the man, husband and father he is to become.

The Underachiever

An "underachiever" can result when mother's, knowingly or unknowingly, place too much of the household burden on a son that is too young and ill prepared. When this happens, the son often ends up as an economic or social underachiever. In the situations I've encountered, the boys that took on too much responsibility early on, whether financial or the role of family protector, has partly resulted in many of them underachieving in their own personal and professional lives, or making a choice to engage in illegal activity to bring in fast cash. I understand that many single mothers are doing well financially, so the financial part of this equation may not be an issue for you. However, if your son is the only male child or the oldest, he may begin to feel a sense of ownership over the family—it is natural. You may not believe this but, as men, we have a natural inclination to take care of our family. It has been said that one of the reasons why so many men fail in this area is simply because, based on history, they don't feel as though they can succeed in doing it. Oftentimes they fear a lack of consistent, sustainable income or simply lack the confidence and discipline to handle the mental, physical, and emotional responsibility that comes with having a family.

I am not making excuses for un-supportive fathers, and I am certainly not making light of a financial situation that can most definitely get tight for some mothers. I actually believe your son should do his fair share around the house. As a matter of fact, it is critical that you assign your son age-appropriate chores and responsibilities, like taking out the trash, washing dishes, cleaning his room, etc. Furthermore, boys who are high-school aged should be encouraged to get some type of part-time job (as long as it doesn't interfere with school or his chosen extra-curricular activity), so that he can gain work experience and feel the confidence of having a little money in his pocket. But, in my opinion, that is where it should end.

When a young man is asked, whether implicitly or explicitly, to help bear the financial responsibility or role of protector in the family, and the outlook never improves, it has been my experience that it can leave him with feelings of failure. Unfortunately, this has left many men in this situation less inclined to try to establish or maintain a household of their own when it is actually time. So it results in him never assuming responsibility for a family, not ever fully engaging or connecting if he does start a family or quitting all-together.

I believe lending an ear when it came to financial matters was my role. Even as early as ten years old, I remember my mother feverishly making phone calls to borrow or make arrangements to cover the bills for a particular month. As I got a little older, she would openly communicate with me the specifics of our financial predicament. I know it was more for moral support, but I felt responsible for providing a solution or at least a little financial relief. At that age, I really couldn't help her financially, so I often felt frustrated. I wasn't alone either, as many of the guys in my neighborhood had a similar financial situation to ours. Some of them let it fuel them to succeed; others resorted to selling drugs or other criminal activity to help out. When I was old enough to make those kinds of choices, by the grace of God I took the positive approach and secured part-time jobs to help to take care of the things I wanted that were above and beyond my basic needs.

In some cultures it is customary for boys to take on added responsibility for the family, I get this. But when your son feels that financing the household or protecting the family has partly become his responsibility, you are setting up a situation that could lead him to neglect or leave school, or could tie him to you in an unhealthy way. I also understand that it does get a little hectic, and your son offers a male perspective, but be conscious of how he may internalize this experience; and if you see him taking on responsibility that he shouldn't, talk to him about what his role in the family is versus what he may be inclined to think or want it to be.

The Drill Sergeant

I know you have met this guy before—a borderline, or maybe over the line, narcissist. Extremely self-centered, this type guy simply has an unrealistic sense of his self-worth. The Drill Sergeant (DS) often comes across as either unaware or unconcerned about his behavior; as a result, many of his relationships are combative. This personality trait seems more common in boys whose mother's tend to heap unrealistic praise and adoration on them. Early in his childhood, he's labeled the 'golden child.' Creating a DS is one of those situations that start harmlessly because this mother, like most parents, is overly concerned about cultivating healthy self-esteem within her child.

Professionally, the Drill Sergeant has just as much of a chance to be an angry failure or wild success. The reason I call him a Drill Sergeant, dates back to early in my career—the guy actually was a graduate of West Point. If you ever worked for or closely with a person like this, you know that they can get a lot done, but will steam roll everyone in the process of doing it, with little regard for the toes they step on. Even though the Drill Sergeant (DS) is praised and commended by his superiors for getting things done; his behavior often times leaves this once promising and extremely bright individual, floundering in a role that is "well below" what everyone thought or expected of him. While this guy can excel in his career in some capacity, the Drill Sergeant typically fails at more intimate relationships and friendships. I have run into the DS most often in the corporate arena, and he normally has a simmering anger and has either never been married or possibly working on his 2nd or 3rd try. The Drill Sergeant typically doesn't fail because he didn't do his job right (even his ex-wives will probably have one or two redeeming qualities they can share about him), he falls short in his style of communication and ability to relate with others. Because, let's face it, when you are told and treated as if you are the most important person in the world, you tend not to be as concerned about other people or their feelings. The Drill Sergeants I know seemed to have been praised most often because of their looks, smarts or some athletic ability. If your son has been blessed in one of these ways, make sure that you place the focus on who your son is as a person, not how well he performs at a certain thing. Also provide him with a balanced perspective about his abilities, because once he leaves home the world certainly will. This new reality can and often does leave the Drill Sergeant angry and out to prove something—and not in a good way.

Momma's Boy

The Momma's Boy is probably the most talked about personality and in some circles, he has reached 'rock star' status. For that reason, I honestly believe more often than not mother's that influence this behavior, do so very innocently. When your son is very young, people may jokingly say that you are spoiling him or that he's a Momma's Boy, because as a small child you probably did spoil him. The problem creeps in if you fail to adjust the dynamics of the relationship as your son matures or you establish ambiguous boundaries for your relationship. If you don't catch it, you will find that you have the same type of relationship with him as an adult as you did when he was a child. Making excuses for his behavior, failing to insist that he take full responsibility for himself and his decisions, or feeling as though he shouldn't make decisions without you, etc. It may sound harmless, but over time, this dynamic can slowly take a toll on his self-confidence. They are not quick to argue or resist this dynamic either, because in his view, the Momma's Boy "has it good." However most men I know that behave like this, begin to doubt themselves and feel justified when they fail to take responsibility for their actions, and in some situations, the lives they wreck or children they create.

As I stated, this type of relationship can happen very innocently. Your job is to make sure that you strike the right balance. I sometimes marvel at the relationship my wife has established with our sons. I tease them a lot and say that she spoils them. However, that couldn't be more from the truth as she is the primary disciplinarian and does a good job balancing her discipline with love. No matter how badly they've behaved, after the punishment has been handed down, they always test her to see how she will respond to them. She has a way of reminding them of their behavior without condemning them as people. She holds them accountable, but reminds them that life is about second chances—in their cases, second, third, and fourth sometimes. She does spoil them a little, but I think the balance of accountability is what she uses to avoid turning them into Momma's Boys. As you can see, this type of relationship is not unique to single mothers, but unfortunately you have the reputation for influencing the behavior most often.

As your son moves into manhood, he should be taught to be independent in both thoughts and actions. His independence is important, as it will help him establish boundaries with others and resist the peer pressure he will inevitably encounter. I know several guys who established this type of relationship with their mother and it was difficult to break away. For example, a friend of mine finally tied the knot when he was 35 or so. Before he got married he was living at home with his mother. Even though the couple moved into their own home and appeared to have established a solid foundation, they announced that they were divorcing roughly one year later. Fortunately, they managed to patch things up and are still married, and have been for several years. However, I recall our conversations during that time and my friend confided that the relationship with his mother had become a little challenging, because he realized that they hadn't established boundaries within their relationship. His mother found reasons for him to stop by her house almost everyday to spend time with her and that he would sometimes oblige her request to accompany him and his wife on dates. I believe his mother felt that he was moving on without her and she used guilt to keep him close. As you can imagine, after a few months of this it started causing conflict with his new wife and he was put in a position where he had to choose.

After many years of trying to navigate opposing relationships, he was finally able to put his relationship with his mother in proper perspective. I understand as we get older the roles of parent and child can be reversed—this was not one of those cases. However, the tangled relationship she'd established with her son almost cost him his marriage and her, a relationship with their three beautiful children. This case may sound extreme, but it is more common than you may think. Remember the relationship you have with your son as he gets older will be a reflection of the relationship you develop with him in childhood. You can have a close relationship with your son, but know where to draw appropriate boundaries and be careful not to alienate him if he begins to draw them for himself. I can think of a lot of things you can help your son to become, but a Momma's Boy shouldn't be one of them.

Henpecked Man

It is a little 'old school,' but we've probably all heard the term and know exactly what it means. Most often this guy is identified by the dynamic between his wife or significant other and him. I have strong evidence that this behavior gets started long before that. What tends to be the case is that he simply selected a mate that highlights this unfortunate characteristic. If you have ever witnessed the interaction between this type of man and his wife it can be a little disturbing. It can be even more unsettling to witness him in the workplace. In this instance, he either serves as the public 'whipping boy' for senior management or he keeps the entire office nervously waiting for the day he finally 'goes off.' In my opinion, this is the most troubling trait the mother/son dynamic can create because his self-respect has been badly damaged. This guy can either come across as if he is over-compensating for pretty much everything or he can be extremely introverted and even a little socially awkward, neither of which is a recipe for success.

I am no psychologist, but I've seen this occur, when boys endure consistently harsh treatment, whether verbal or physical, at the hands of their mother. I know at times either parent, not just mothers, under stress or short on patience can discipline in a way that could be considered harsh. Therefore, I recommend that you consciously approach discipline using a variety of ways. Because boys in particular will require that you employ a variety of tools to get your point across. Consistently harsh treatment is not the way. If you are not sure how your interactions are affecting him, just watch him with others. His behavior with a peer will most likely mirror the dynamic between the two of you. If he is very docile with you but overly aggressive with others or he gets dominated easily, it may be worth taking a step back to consider what may be taking place. When the dynamics of your relationship result in this behavior, it can manifest itself in ways described above or an unhealthy dependence on you. In some cases, I've witnessed men grow to resent their mothers or act out in extremely destructive ways.

Just remember as men, it is instinctive for us to want to express our dominance and challenge boundaries. I'm not suggesting that you relinquish control of your household, but be careful not to create an unnecessary barrier between you and your son. Give him a little rope and pull him back when needed. In short—learn to pick your battles. If you don't, my experience is that by taking a more dominant approach you will likely inhibit his independence and desire to assert himself in any number of ways.

....

The section primarily serves to remind you to be aware of the dynamic you are creating between you and your son. How are the interactions between you unfolding? The best rule of thumb is to treat your son with respect and always have the goal of creating a man that has all the qualities you would want in a husband and father for your children. Looking at it from that perspective will help you recalibrate your relationship when necessary.

Given the time constraints you may find yourself in, it will be easy to fall back on a way of relating with your son that is easy; and let's face it, showing a child mutual respect, after a long day at work, is not always an easy thing to do. However, I did tell you that shepherding your son through the strategies within each priority would require work, but I can guarantee that it will result in the exact outcome you want for him—success. Most successful men share several common characteristics, with the most notable being self-confidence. Being an Underachiever, Drill Sergeant, Momma's Boy or being referred to as a Henpecked Man won't get him there!

Chapter 3

Develop Lasting Relationships with Others Including His Father

Highlights	
"A young man's ability to gather the social skills necessary to interact effectively will play a big role in how he feels about himself and how he connects with others."	
– Managing a Complicated Relationship with His Dad – Building Relationships with Others	– When You Have a Significant Other – Help Him Manage Conflict

Essential to building healthy long-term relationships is learning how to interact well with others. How your son feels about himself will be a key factor in how successful he is making and maintaining friendships or simply managing day-to-day interactions with others. When he has a solid, balanced relationship with you, it is more likely that his confidence will reflect that. Another key to healthy relationships is his ability to communicate his thoughts and feelings appropriately. In Chapter 1, we discussed the importance of your son finding his own voice. When he finds his own voice, identifying the right types of friendships to hold on to—or not, will be much easier.

Most boys would not be considered overly social. However, his ability to gather the social skills necessary to interact effectively with others will play a big role in how he feels about himself, and how he is perceived. Fair or not, the world judges us by how well we relate with others and how well we can articulate our thoughts. It is important not to take social skills for granted and expect them to just appear for your son. Carrying a conversation, managing conflict, or connecting with people on a deeper level requires social skills. I am not suggesting that he has to be the "the life of the party," but there are many levels before that. So it is important to look for opportunities to build the social skills he needs. If it is difficult for him to connect, he may have a hard time being accepted by his peers. When this happens I've seen kids turn to a number of places to get the acceptance they crave; whether it is negative behavior or hanging out with the wrong crowd.

This chapter will focus on the final pieces of the puzzle to establishing healthy relationships. *First, I address the importance of the relationship between your son and his father and how you can help him navigate the challenges that may bring. Next, how you can help him establish and maintain relationships with others is also discussed. Thirdly, I walk you through what to consider when you introduce a new significant other into the picture; and finally, I have identified strategies to support the critical skill of managing conflicts in his relationships.*

Managing a Complicated Relationship with His Dad

I believe most fathers play or would like to play an important role in their children's lives, especially a son. Whether through circumstance or bad choices, sometimes the relationship never progresses to a meaningful place. If your son's father is actively engaged in his life, count him blessed. I say this realizing that there are many healthy father/son relationships out there, where the father is very engaged. If he is not, make sure that you are not a barrier to them establishing a meaningful relationship. Go a step further and ensure that you are doing all you can to encourage his involvement. For those fathers that aren't involved or represent a negative distraction, you may ask yourself, "How can I help this situation?" or "Do I really want to encourage this?" Not to mention managing your own thoughts about your son's father. However if your primary goal is to develop your son into a successful man, it is critically important that he reconcile his feelings about his father. Your role in this case is to help your son determine what his expectation should be as it relates to future interactions or establishing a longer-term relationship with his father. When expectations are set appropriately it minimizes disappointments. Also help your son get clarity about his feelings regarding his father. It will do more to help his inner strength than I can explain in this book.

If you are successful helping him come to terms with the relationship he can have with his father, it will make your job helping him establish and manage relationships with others much easier.

There's no doubt that your son experiences a number of emotions related to the absence of his father. I was angry, but I didn't really understand the magnitude of my feelings. When he was paroled, I was 15 years old. I was actually pretty excited about him coming back despite my anger. In my mind, I felt that once he came back we would be a 'real' family and things would finally settle down—well they didn't. After he got out, I assume due to the passing of so much time, he and my mother never re-established their relationship. A few years later they legally divorced. It took some time, but I slowly established a relationship with him and came to terms with my feelings. Once that bond was established, it really was a liberating feeling. For this reason, I am a firm believer that as long as he is not a detriment, you should leave the door open for your son to have a relationship with his father. Once I started my own family, my children came to know and really care about him. My father passed away just after my 40th birthday and when I think about him, I feel great joy because I turned my anger into empathy for his struggle and found peace with that aspect of my life. My father and I were certainly responsible for the way our relationship turned out, but I credit my mother for never putting him down in front of us and always encouraging us to establish some kind of relationship with him.

Growing up, my grandmother would tell me, "If you can't respect the man, respect the position." I really didn't understand what that meant at the time, but as I have matured, I am amazed by the number of times I have had to recall those words. Of course it came to mind many times in my professional life, but it was also a perspective I had to take as it pertained to my father. He deserved a lot of things...but early on, respect was not one of them. The situation with your son's father may call for this perspective too. I know for some of you, respect is the farthest thing from your mind, but be careful not to disrespect your son's father in front of him because he represents something important to your son and he is part of him. You don't want him to internalize the negative language you use to refer to his father or any other man for that matter, and feel that it also applies to him. I think you can more easily understand the negative repercussions of being disrespectful or using negative language about his father.

However there are two situations that you may find yourself in as it relates to you, your son and his father, where emotions could run high. While not as obvious as the situation mentioned above, they can be just as counter-productive to the relationship:

1)   He Has a Significant Other – First of all, the more positive people your son can have in his life, the better. So I would hope you take that approach as it relates to your son's father and his new wife or significant other. If your son's father has a significant other—respect that and be careful not to become a negative force. This is often masked as a mother's desire to 'protect' her child. You can easily slip into this trap, because let's face it, these situations can be emotionally charged. However if you find yourself using disparaging remarks, insinuating—but not really saying, that her behavior is somehow detrimental to your son—please refrain. If this sounds familiar, there is a chance you could be guilty of this behavior—especially if you haven't addressed your concerns with your son's father or his significant other.

There certainly have been and will continue to be instances where you need to make sure everyone is behaving respectfully, your son included. However if you think it is a true problem, confront it. The long and short of it is that you should want the relationship with anyone involved with your son to be positive. This person could do positive things in his life and actually serve as an ally for you, and encourage your child's father to support him in a positive way. So be careful not to create a negative situation where there isn't one. I know all too well about mothers who take this position. Your son is going to follow your lead and could miss out on having a relationship with someone who could be extremely helpful to both of you.

2)   The Relationship Is Not about Money – The second type of situation I would caution you to guard against is the temptation to marginalize your son's father as merely a means for financial support. If your son's father is contributing financially, be appreciative and yes respectful. I understand it is his responsibility to help you support your son financially and if he is not supporting I am the first to tell you that you should go through the proper channels to ensure that he owns up to his responsibility. However, your appreciation for his financial

support or the time he spends with your son demonstrates a bigger lesson we should teach our children. The lesson is about appreciation regardless of the situation.

Fathers can and should serve an extremely important role for their children. When you connect the father's significance to only being financial, you reduce his ability to be an effective parent. There are going to be times when your son will not listen to you. The second most important relationship in his life should be his father. You don't want him to be able to only get your son's attention when he's handing out money – because he won't have his attention very long.

Also if your son's father cannot pay or provide support; for the sake of your son, avoid the temptation to connect your eagerness to help establish a relationship between the two of them with his willingness or ability to provide financial support. I certainly am not condoning it, but do understand that a father's inability to pay may be the result of a number of reasons. The reasons may or may not be justified to you. However, it is important that fathers are allowed to be involved in their children's lives if they are not a detriment and want to be.

In some cases, you need to be ready to help prepare your son for the unfortunate reality that a relationship with his father may not be possible right now. If you find yourself in this situation, make sure that your concern for your son's feelings aren't leading you to compound his emotional distress by making negative comments about his father. This is a critically important time that you have to assume the duty of mentor and not mother. You can be very influential to the relationship your son could have with his father in the future. Stay in communication with your son about his feelings, and if he comes to the conclusion that a relationship with his father is not possible, he will need you to help him grieve for the relationship he wanted, but also remain open to the possibility that at some point down the road having a relationship may be an option. Take it from me, making a connection with your father, after a long estrangement is possible. If you can help him work through his feelings, it is a step that can help heal places in your son's heart that he is unaware are broken.

Building Relationships with Others

I remember when most neighborhoods came with built-in opportunities for socialization and the best place to meet and make friends was on the playground. Times are a little different today. Now, with less time and more skepticism about people, many of us are opting to allow Xbox® or PlayStation® to fill the void. In some communities parents still monitor their child's interactions by scheduling specific play dates with other neighborhood children. Although taking these steps makes us much more comfortable with whom our children interact, this approach can sanitize the social experience. As your son gets older, school will help to fill the void in some ways, but as soon as the bell rings, everyone will go on with their over-scheduled lives, or go home to do homework and…you guessed it, play video games. If this sounds like your life, here are a few strategies you should consider as you seek to get more meaningful social interaction for your son:

1) Find Ways to Engage – Get your son involved in activities that will allow him to interact with others, and use the activity as an opportunity to build his social skills--for example, Boy Scouts, Boys Club, or team sports, etc. For many working parents, managing the logistics of getting your son to and from activities can be tough. Try your best to be creative. Consider car-pooling with other parents or ask the leader of the activity for assistance. I have found that with team sports, in particular, the level of support you receive from the coaches and other parents is high.

2) Get Comfortable – Encourage your son to interact with others as much as possible and in different settings. The more he does this, the more comfortable he'll become and the more experience he'll gain with a variety of people. For example, have him try something he's never done. If he's not a chess player, enroll him in a course that will teach him how to play the game and he will meet a host of boys around his age.

3) Talk it Out – Talk with your son about the interactions he has with others and help him understand the dynamics of the conversations. Help him identify and understand different social cues. For example, recognizing when someone is being sarcastic,

or knowing when you've worn out your welcome. Also, consider role-playing with your son, as it will help him generate the best responses to social situations and will prepare him to know what to do or how to communicate his thoughts.

4) Pay Attention – This goes without saying, but be on the lookout and identify areas where he may have difficulty socially and discuss ways he can manage through it or minimize his discomfort.

When You Have a Significant Other

Families are about inclusion. If you are trying to establish a family or parameters for a new relationship, everyone has to be included in the discussion. There is no such thing as separate but equal, in well-functioning relationships. Make sure the three of you sit down together and gain an agreement on how the relationship will operate. Also, in private, reassure your son that no one is trying to take his father's place, and that you certainly aren't going anywhere. I think change is the scariest thing for kids in this situation. As for your significant other, as long as boundaries have been established he should be fine. I believe the situation gets a little muddy when those involved feel overlooked, including your significant other. Once everyone knows the 'rules of the road,' let your son's father know that you have introduced someone new into your son's life, and that any support would be appreciated. If your son's father is mature he should handle this with no problem. The least he can do is be supportive and try to promote a positive relationship for all involved. However, if he doesn't take a supportive approach you cannot do anything about the 'back-chatter' or negative things he may say to your son. The best way to combat this is for you and your significant other to stay positive and consistent with the agreement the three of you have established. Another way to keep the relationship positive is to keep the lines of communication open in all directions.

Also, be careful not to force the situation between your significant other and your son. You have to give them time to establish their relationship. Men tend to bond in unexpected and subtle ways. When they are given the opportunity to share alone time at a sporting event or over a chess game, their relationship will have a better chance of developing. So give them time and allow things to progress naturally. While I encourage you to have a life outside of being a mother, before you introduce anyone new to your son, be certain you know him and his motives well. Introducing anyone new, especially men to your son can be tricky. Again I stress, keep the lines of communication open enough so that your son feels free to communicate any concerns. I believe the 'right' kind of new people can represent a breath of fresh air for you and your son. Just as I mentioned, when your son's father introduces a new partner, the same goes for you; any positive relationship is a good one for your son and you too.

Help Him Manage Conflict

Webster defines conflict as a, mental (or physical) struggle resulting from incompatible or opposing needs, drives, wishes, or external or internal demands. Based on that definition, there can be many opportunities for conflict to occur and it will come in different shapes and forms and with different people. As pointed out a little earlier, having the ability to work through conflict and manage difficult people and situations is one of the most important skills your son can learn. When he enters the business arena, the need for conflict management will be a daily occurrence. Having the skills to manage through these experiences will be critically important to how far your son climbs the corporate ladder, or any ladder for that matter. However today, this skill will help him preserve the important relationships in his life, and in more challenging instances, it can help him avoid a dangerous situation.

Unfortunately, there will be times when your son's 'manhood' will be tested. Other boys and eventually men will challenge him; it is in our nature. However, it doesn't always require that he fights his way out of it. The critical thing is that your son clearly understands that this is just one of many options he has to consider when dealing with the spectrum of conflict that ranges from harmless to very aggressive.

Conflict can also arise from competition and as you know, boys tend to be competitive. This competitiveness will most likely be the source of most of your son's conflict. In my opinion, his first line of defense should always be, to take a humble approach. When a man separates his wins or losses from his ego or who he is as a person, and feels confident about the effort he puts in, he won't be as compelled to brag about his wins or become upset when he loses. If you talk to him about humility in those terms and share with him how he should behave in competitive situations; your son will probably take on this posture as he matures. Consider sharing this series of strategies to help him work through conflict with others:

1) Listen – Everyone has a point of view. *Listen* to the other person first. Gandhi said it best, "Seek first to understand then to be understood."

2) Acknowledge – Always a*cknowledge* how the other person feels. Empathy is one emotion that is in short supply. If your son is going to take the step to listen to the other person's point of view, he should demonstrate the next step by letting them know he heard their point.

3) Re-state Problem – Have your son *reiterate* what the source of the conflict is. Too often, people have conflict, but are unclear as to what they are in conflict about. Make sure that your son understands the importance of recognizing and communicating what he thinks is the source of the problem.

4) Explain Position – Your son should understand and be able to *explain* his position. This step gives him just enough time to stop and think about why his position is important, why he is invested in his position, and to what degree is his position important?

5) Compromise – Try to work out a *compromise* that is agreeable to both parties; a solution that hopefully allows everyone to come away with something they wanted. If you cannot reach a win/win agreement, your son has to be prepared to determine how important his position is to him. Is he more concerned with winning or is he strongly tied to his point of view for reasons of right and wrong? If it isn't as important this time, he should allow the other person to have their way. However, if he is just as tied to his opinion as the other person, he can close off the discussion by saying something like, "Each person deserves his or her opinion and it is probably best to move on to something else."

If your son gets into a heated exchange with a friend, family member, or classmate, everyone will most likely demonstrate reasonable behavior and together, will most likely find effective ways to resolve the conflict. On the other hand, when your son encounters unreasonable people who at times may also be a friend, family member, or classmate, most likely he will only have two options; to either walk away, or stay and debate. Unfortunately, if your son chooses to stay and debate, he has to be prepared and know that tensions may escalate the situation into something physical. I certainly don't advocate for fighting, however, as I said in the earlier section, there may come a time when no amount of debate or rationalization will help, and the other person takes that aggressive step toward your son. Just have him be prepared for this, because the downfall in allowing him to freely interact with others is that more negative interactions are possible. Regardless of the outcome, he should be able to look at the conflict and learn from it.

. . . .

Remember, building healthy long-term relationships is all about learning how to interact well with others. Your son's ability to relate with others will be a key part of his future success and plays a huge role in how others perceive him, how successful he is at making and maintaining friendships, or how he manages his day-to-day interactions. Allow the process to happen naturally, but do offer as many opportunities as possible for your son to get social interaction.

Priority 2

Achieve 'Self' Mastery for Strong Character

"Watch your thoughts, for they become words. Watch your words, for they become actions. Watch your actions, for they become habits. Watch your habits, for they become character. Watch your character, for it becomes your destiny."

Author Unknown

For the most part, this book is about Success and how you as a parent can give your son the best chance to achieve it. What I have found in my experience as a father, mentor and employer is that the biggest 'barrier' that gets in the way of our success, once all other factors are accounted for, is—ourselves. There are already enough obstacles your son will have to navigate, so let's make sure he's not getting in his own way. In *Priority 1*, I identified how your son can establish the kinds of relationships that will offer stability and instill the confidence necessary to take bigger and bolder steps in his life. Having that stability will make it easier for him to become the man he wants to be, starting on the inside and working his way out. For this reason, *Priority 2* focuses on helping him to achieve 'self-mastery,' in three critical areas. Your son's ability to achieve mastery will hinge on him becoming more aware of his thoughts and actions, and as a result be better able to manage his behavior and the choices he makes.

This priority will get into what I consider to be the core components of a man's character—*Self-Discipline, Self-Respect, and Self-Direction*. Helping him achieve mastery in these areas will take time and patience, and having a solid partnership will put you in the best position to do it. If your son is able to master *Self-Discipline he will possess the appropriate level of self-control and be able to focus on what he is trying to achieve in life. With healthy Self-Respect your son's behavior will consistently reflect his values, and being Self-Directed will give your son the tools to make good decisions and be prepared to take responsibility for them.* While it certainly will be up to your son to take the actual steps, I am directing the conversation to you because there are several strategies you will be able to employ to get or keep him on the path to mastering 'self.'

Many of the troubling statistics I discussed earlier in this book can be directly attributed to the failure of our boys to achieve self-mastery. Conversely, when you examine men of strong character, that have also achieved high levels of success, you will be able to quickly determine that they've mastered all of these traits, specifically in the area they found success. I suspect that to achieve mastery, these individuals had to have a high level of self awareness. When your son possesses awareness of himself, it will give him the ability to recognize how other people perceive him and will help him monitor his attitudes as well as how and why he responds to what is going on in a given moment. Your son's level of awareness will directly impact his ability to achieve mastery in these areas. I suggest that during his day-to-day routine, pay close attention to his behavior in a way that helps to determine how aware he is of his own thoughts and behaviors. Point out if you notice any recurring behaviors, and offer solutions that will support his effort to achieve mastery of 'self.' The reason I mention this, is because most men, especially those raised without the benefit of a father—if they are honest – will tell you that they experience a lot of internal dialogue to determine what actions to take and the decisions to make. If as parents we can shape the conversation that goes on in the minds of our sons, it will be a huge step toward making them more aware of those thoughts and the resulting actions.

Chapter 4

Self-Discipline Underlies Success

Highlights
"The key to instilling self-discipline in boys lies in a parent's ability to provide a consistently structured environment."

– Set Boundaries with Family Rules	– Reward Good Behavior & Establish Consequences
– Turn off the Television	

For children, boys especially, self-discipline is supremely important and will give them the poise needed to succeed in all areas of life. Mastery of self-discipline is a habitual process and can only happen over time—the result of consistent and intentioned effort. It is much easier to support this process with children because they haven't had the time to develop bad habits that have to be undone. As the saying goes, "children are like sponges", well let's ensure that our boys soak up the discipline they need to drive their success later in life. The rewards associated with achieving self-discipline and being disciplined can't be overstated! When you look at the following list of exceptional men, whether you agree with all aspects of their behavior, politics or personality or not, is unimportant. What has to be acknowledged is that an incredible level of discipline has underscored their overwhelming success – and they happen to have all been raised by a single mother; President Barack Obama, President Bill Clinton, Justice Clarence Thomas, Alan Greenspan, Ben Carson, Bill Cosby, Les Brown, Jackie Robinson, Troy Aikman, Lance Armstrong, Michael Phelps, Tom Cruise, Quentin Tarintino and even music mogul Jay Z. While he began his assent to success in a non-traditional way, his story is no less important. Even early on, Jay Z was disciplined enough to identify a path to success and stick with it. It has been said that he would spend hours studying the dictionary to learn new words and understand their meaning, which in part helps him deliver thought provoking lyrics. It takes discipline to study your craft and develop extraordinary skills.

In the best-selling book *Outliers: The Story of Success* by Malcolm Gladwell, he proposes that the key to success in any field is in large part a matter of practicing a task for around 10,000 hours. From my own experiences with drumming I believe this to be correct. I know I had to have logged at least that many hours by the time I was a senior in High School. To log those types of hours it takes an incredible amount of discipline. I share this to underscore the importance of identifying your son's talents early and encouraging him to dedicate himself to working toward clocking those hours—whether 10,000, 2,000, or somewhere in between. The ultimate payoff of self-discipline is focus. When your son can maintain laser-like focus on the challenges and tasks he faces, success, is just around the corner.

What I have come to realize is the key to building self-discipline is consistency and being in a consistently structured environment. For some busy parents, staying locked into a schedule or creating a more ordered existence might seem rigid or difficult to do given the demands placed on you. So for those mothers, I offer a suggestion. Think about how you feel when your workday is turned upside down, and everything your boss is asking you to do is disorganized and not completely thought through. I don't know about you, but I would feel very frustrated. The reality is that many of us, not just single mothers, ask our boys to operate in this kind of environment most days and expect it to yield success for them. I'm not saying your situation is that dramatic, but providing the predictability of a structured day for your son will benefit him in the same way it benefits adults.

If you think your family could use a little tune-up, consider the following strategies as ways to bring more structure to the way you operate day-to-day:

Set Boundaries with Family Rules

Setting boundaries for your son is an important aspect of building discipline and helping him understand what is acceptable and what is not. It is a necessary part of the training he needs to become a disciplined man. The best way to establish boundaries is through the use of family rules. Rules should be specific, clear and easy for your son to understand. When you establish rules, they should be achievable, age appropriate and enforced consistently. During the process of establishing the family rules, I would highly recommend that you include your son. He is more likely to adhere to them if he agreed to them up front, and understands why they are needed.

Turn off the Television

Your son may think that of all the ideas you will present to him, the notion of turning off the television is probably the most radical. Nevertheless, I strongly believe that when we limit our children's screen activity, it can help improve mental clarity and force them to be more creative thinkers. There may not be any science behind what I am saying, but there have always been movements that advocate a zero tolerance for television. I wouldn't go that far because I believe like with everything, if we monitor what they watch, listen to, and log on to, we can let them indulge in moderation. However, I do recommend no more than 30 minutes per day of screen activity (includes television, computer, video game, etc.), on school nights. Additional time can be negotiated on the weekends. The obvious exception would be the time required to complete schoolwork. I also suggest that televisions and computers be limited to common areas of your home. Hopefully this is already old news to you and you have already limited your son's screen time. If not, you should be able to point to several ways we discuss in the book to engage his time – projects, extra-curricular activities and household chores—just to name a few.

Reward Good Behavior & Establish Consequences

I am a big proponent of giving rewards for good behavior. In general, I believe most children would naturally prefer to be acknowledged for what they do well. Take this notion a step further and consider establishing a system for rewarding your son. For example, prepare a reward chart and discuss ahead of time what behaviors warrant which type of reward.

Just as you need to reward him for good behavior, you must also be prepared to establish consequences for bad behavior. It is also best to think through specific consequences ahead of time so that they can be imposed when an infraction occurs. Remember penalties for undesirable behavior should be specific and clearly explained—I would suggest starting with a warning. Consequences do not need to be harsh or severe to be effective. Generally, if consequences are too harsh, resentment, defiance and power struggles are frequently the result. As long as consequences are reasonable they are generally more effective, especially if you let your son negotiate some of them.

. . . .

As discussed in this chapter, the lack of self-discipline can show up in a number of ways: poor grades, drug abuse, and criminal activity, being unfaithful to a spouse, or engaging in violent behavior. In fact, the lack of self-discipline has caused several of my colleagues to say and do things in the workplace that they couldn't recover from. Do what it takes to ensure that your son doesn't have a similar fate. It will take time, but do what is necessary to create a structured environment for your son and help him directly by becoming the best example of discipline he can have. You may think your son doesn't notice and he may go so far as to try to minimize your impact. Perhaps it's a 'boy' thing, but don't be fooled—you are his most important role model and a real-time, walking, talking example of responsibility and self-discipline.

Chapter 5

Self-Respect Determines Your Standards

Highlights
"High standards are often the result of healthy Self Respect. Your standards reflect what you are willing to accept in terms of your own behavior as well as how you expect others to treat you."

– Be a Model of Self-Respect For Your Son – Teach Him to Demonstrate Self Love	– Encourage Him to Connect to Something Bigger Than Himself

At a very basic level, self-respect really boils down to whether you like yourself or not. When we have a strong and genuine sense of who we are, we feel empowered to define and live by our own values. In helping your son build his Self-Respect, you want him to accept himself just as he is and appreciate his connection to this world and place in it. He shouldn't need the approval of others and he shouldn't measure his self-worth based on someone else's yardstick. Make every effort to help him gain a genuine appreciation for who he is and what he can become at a very early age. Not in ambiguous terms, but actually working with him to identify what makes him unique.

High standards are also the result of healthy Self-Respect. Your standards reflect what you are willing to accept in terms of your own behavior as well as how you expect others to treat you. People with a healthy self-respect live by the golden rule, "Do unto others as you would have them do unto you." As your son matures, you will find another measure of how he feels about himself, is that he will have a personal standard for the type of work he produces and will give 100%

of his effort; especially for those things he is passionate about. Take a look at the following ways I believe will help you engage your son in building a healthy sense of self:

Be a Model of Self-Respect for Your Son

Your son will watch how you treat yourself. Do you proactively take care of your health, happiness and finances? Also are you conscious of your negative self-talk and the way you present yourself in public. Your son will watch how you treat him too. Do you use words to affirm him? Have you provided structure and consistency in his life? The way you treat him will go a long way to promoting a healthy self-respect.

Teach Him to Demonstrate Self Love

He has to make a habit of reminding himself of his positive attributes. It is one thing for someone else to affirm you, but if your son is countering it with negative self-talk, it won't matter. I have identified suggestions you can consider as a way to remind him of the great kid he is and diminish any negative thoughts he has about himself or his abilities:

1) Encourage him to associate with positive, supportive people. Given your geography or other circumstances, your son may be in a position where he feels isolated or alone. Some friends are better than no friends, right? Wrong. I encourage you to seek avenues to get him positive interactions with others, but you should also be prepared to keep reminding him of the benefits of being his own person. When we first moved to the Northeast and hadn't met many people, I would often tell my oldest son that sometimes, "God sets us apart from others because he has a special plan that he is preparing us for and others may get in the way of that plan." He may have experienced moments of loneliness after our talk, but he also felt special as he referenced back to it often.

2) Help him make a list of his past successes and positive attributes. The list doesn't necessarily have to consist of monumental accomplishments. It can include small victories like learning to ride a bike, working hard to bring up a grade, specific sports

achievements, receiving an award, etc. He should keep the list in a place where he can recall it often.

3)   The world won't come to an end if he makes a mistake, or two, or three.   Help him understand that he has to learn from his mistakes, but more importantly, he must forgive himself and move on.

4)   Give him the opportunity to be his own man. This is so very important, as we discussed in Chapter 1, support his effort to *Find His Own Voice*. When he can do that, he learns to honor himself and act in accordance with what he thinks he is all about.

Encourage Him to Connect to Something Bigger than Himself

Help him get connected. The easiest and best opportunity for connection is through religious services. I would highly recommend that you join a local church, synagogue or mosque, to interact with individuals that have common values. In addition to religious services, there are also a number of other things your son can do to feel that he is part of something bigger than him. Small gestures matter! He can help an elderly person with his or her grocery bags, hold the door open for a stranger or volunteer to work for a non-profit organization. The point is to recognize opportunities to assist others and offer your services voluntarily. Doing for others will lead him to a greater awareness of things and people around him which will ultimately help him connect with the spiritual concept of being part of something much bigger and grander than he.

. . . .

If you were to discount every other aspect of this book and place all your effort on supporting your son in mastering the lone characteristic of self-respect, it could have a profound ripple -effect on our collective society. If a greater number of boys were to care more about themselves and as a consequence care more about others, it would immediately impact the rates of suicide and violent crimes against others.

Chapter 6

Self-Direction is Critical for Decision-Making

<table>
<tr><td colspan="2" align="center">Highlights</td></tr>
<tr><td colspan="2">"Our lives, in large part, are shaped by the choices we make and teaching your son to make good ones will be critical to his future success."</td></tr>
<tr><td>– ED Can Help Make Decisions Easier (Evaluate, Determine Options, Get Clarity, Ask for Help, Now Decide)</td><td>– Prepare Him to Make Big Choices (Sex, Drugs, Violence and Law Enforcement)</td></tr>
</table>

You will be presented with opportunities to teach your son different life skills at different points along your journey together. The process will begin early and probably last long after he leaves home. Chief among those skills should be helping him develop strategies, to make decisions that are based on his values and beliefs. Our lives, in large part, are shaped by the choices we make and teaching your son to make good ones will be a critical aspect of his development. As your son grows and matures so will the number of choices he has to make as well as their complexity. My sons and I developed a methodical approach to making decisions—ED CAN! It may sound a little corny, but it is very easy for them to remember and has resulted in them taking responsibility for their decisions more quickly, even when the outcome isn't so good. I believe this is the case primarily because they felt they were prepared to make the best possible decision. We joke with each other and say, "If you don't think you can make the right decision, just remember, ED CAN." It may seem like 5 long steps—and who has that much time to make decisions—but as my son has gotten older, he can zip through this in a split second, in most instances.

ED CAN Help Make Decisions Easier

E)   Evaluate the Situation – Identify the situation and take a few minutes to determine if you need to make a choice and why it is necessary to make a choice in the first place.

D)   Determine Options – Determine what your choices are after evaluating the situation. If you are faced with only one alternative, it is pretty simple. However, I have found that most of the time, we have multiple options. The point of the exercise is to make sure he thinks through all his options and the consequences that will result from each one.

C)   Get Clarity – Have clarity about what outcome you want. When you know your options and are clear about the consequences, making the decision boils down to choosing the option that allows you to achieve your desired outcome. Or in some instances choosing the option that gets you closest to what you want.

A)   Ask for Help – Does he hesitate before making a decision? If he thinks he needs to ask for help, encourage him to do so. It is a wise man that will ask for help—no need to flounder if help is within reach.

N)   Now Decide – Don't be afraid. Go ahead and make a decision. You have thought it through and the outcome you desire is possible; so go for it!

With maturity your son will be able to quickly walk through a decision-making process like ED CAN. The confidence he will have in his ability to make sound decisions will result in him becoming less susceptible to negative influences or "peer pressure." When it comes to making decisions, both of you have to remember that it will take some trial and error. Every successful person has made choices they regret. The trick is to learn something from it, and try not to make the mistake again! As his mother, you are in the best position to encourage him to practice a little self-discipline by using a methodical approach. However all the tips and tricks in the world won't amount to much if your son doesn't also take responsibility for the choices, he makes.

On my journey I have been astounded by the number of individuals, men and women, who fail to take responsibility for their decisions and actions. Unfortunately for boys raised by single mothers, the most prominent example of how a man handles responsibility is his father. Therefore, how his father is handling the situation with the two of you will play a role in shaping your son's view of what being a responsible man is. Regardless of that situation, you are still tasked with making sure your son is willing to take responsibility. This is another reason why it is so important that you refrain from making excuses for your son's behavior. Maturity should certainly play a role; however, it has been my experience that when a young man feels he was able to make an informed decision, he is much more willing to accept the consequences for the choices he makes. Whether you share with your son your own method for decision-making or use the ED CAN method; make sure he has the tools he needs to make more thoughtful decisions.

While I take a very mature approach to this type of behavior today, it wasn't always this way. As I mentioned earlier, I was planning for college graduation when I found out I was going to become a father. Having a kid was the last thing on my mind. I was angry because I felt that the birth control thing was being taken care of, later I found out it wasn't. Because I felt the choice was taken away from me, I tried to rationalize why I had the right not to take responsibility for what was about to happen. Once I came to my senses, I realized that it really didn't matter about fault, a kid was coming soon and we were both responsible. A great friend of mine helped me turn the corner when he forced me to see that I did make a choice because I could have been more diligent to ensure this didn't happen. After her birth and years of helping to care for her, I realized that the situation actually grounded me and ultimately made me a stronger person and a better father for her and my two sons. She is in her early twenties now and I enjoy a great relationship with her that will continue to grow and get better and better. My story had a positive ending but my behavior didn't happen overnight—it took time.

Prepare Him to Make Big Choices

As parents, we give our children generic responses or general ways to manage decision-making. However, when it comes to the big choices your son will be faced with, such as whether he should have sex as a teenager or engage in casual drugs with his friends. Arm him with your thoughts on the matter including strategies how he could respond or think about the situation if he finds himself in it. As with any delicate subject, good communication is the key. Having a relationship with your child that is based on trust and open communication will help you stay on top of these tough issues. Remember, start dialogue early, and adjust your conversation as age appropriate. Here are a few thoughts you can consider, to get the dialogue started and will help you both work through these big decisions.

Sex

Choices: Should I Have Sex? Where Can I Get More Information About Sex? How Can I Avoid Some of the Negative Consequences?

Thoughts for Discussion

Some exposure to sex cannot be avoided—sexually tinged images are all around your son, turn on the television, look at a magazine, hop on the Internet—you get the picture! Talking to your son about sex and some of the real life challenges having sex can present, demands an ongoing flow of information that should begin with you and at as early an age as possible. Begin by ensuring that your son understands the biological aspects of the body and sex. Most schools offer health courses by 5th or 6th grade to discuss the basics, but make sure you weigh in on the conversation too.

When it comes to having sex, the easy message is to say, "Wait until marriage," but as he gets older, the likelihood of him adhering to that message is slim. Also, if he is available, let his father weigh in on the conversation, because he may offer a slightly different perspective than yours. Listed below are some specific points you should cover and a few thoughts about each:

Use a Condom – When you talk about condoms, the first thing you should share with your son is that he should not rely on the young lady to provide them. If he is having sex or thinks he wants to, he should have his own protection. There are a number of reasons why he should have his own protection; HIV, sexually transmitted diseases, and unplanned pregnancies.

Having a child out of wedlock is certainly not the worst consequence of unprotected sex; however the reality is that this situation does place an unfair burden on the child that is brought into this world. Not only should your son understand his physical and emotional responsibilities as a possible father, but also when you think it is age appropriate, put pen to paper and show your son the financial implications of having a child.

Also, have a candid conversation with your son about all forms of sexual activity. I know that kids have started to split hairs on defining what sex really is, so make sure you cover the gamut. No matter what

Sex

Choices: Should I Have Sex? Where Can I Get More Information About Sex? How Can I Avoid Some of the Negative Consequences?

you call it, they all present potential dangers for your son and he has to be reminded.

Sex is Emotional – Another reality of sex is dealing with the emotions involved. You may not like hearing this, but for most men, sex is not overly emotional, but, simply a natural biologic function. However the young lady probably won't see things that way. Help him understand that, sex can become extremely emotional for young ladies and depending on the age it may be very difficult for either of them to handle this type of relationship.

He should be sensitive to this. He is also going to watch very closely how you relate with men, his father included. It goes without saying that you should always keep it classy, but you should also guard against introducing too many men into his life, or allowing him to witness you involved in disrespectful relationships. I am not suggesting that you cannot have a life, just be careful to send the right messages as it relates to relationships and how he should treat women.

'No' Means 'No' – If he is intent on having sex, your son has to be able to manage the clues the young lady could be giving him. There have been many instances where young men became involved in legal situations that could have been avoided. Therefore it is critically important that he respects the word 'No' and understands the consequences when he cannot demonstrate self control or good judgment.

Drugs and Alcohol

Choices: Should I Try It? Do I Want To Come Across Looking Like a Baby? What Can I Do To Take The Pain Away?

Thoughts for Discussion

A conversation about the use of drugs and alcohol is also critically important. I think this conversation is probably similar in importance and timing to the discussion you will have about Sex. Drugs and alcohol are readily available to most kids, even in the very best of neighborhoods. Your son has to be comfortable saying 'No,' and be prepared with a variety of ways he can express it. You should work with your son to find appropriate ways to communicate this without feeling alienated by his peers. Many elementary and middle schools have drug prevention programs and do a lot of role-playing to help in this effort. Find out if your son's school has one. If they do, make sure he is involved and take the extra step to follow-up with him and ask questions about what he's learning. Ensure that he knows how you feel about drugs and alcohol—zero tolerance. We know all too well, the path of drugs and alcohol: loss of opportunities, addiction, incarceration, and possibly death. The kids that tend to indulge, especially early are typically crying out for attention or dealing with some pain and cannot express it verbally. As parents we have to ensure that we alleviate those concerns, by keeping the lines of communication open. However the other reason boys may indulge is that he has too much free time on his hands. We have offered a long list of ways to occupy his time—so keep him busy.

Drinking & Driving – When it comes to alcohol especially, even though you have a zero-tolerance policy, you have to make sure your son knows that if he slips, he should never drink and drive. It is more important that he remain safe than worry about getting a lecture from you. Therefore, if he does slip and have a few beers one night at a party, he should not be afraid to call you to pick him up. He should also know to never get in the car with someone else that has been drinking. Too many promising young lives continue to be cut short by getting behind the wheel of a car after a night of drinking. My point with all of this is that you should help give him some parameters to

Drugs and Alcohol

Choices: Should I Try It? Do I Want To Come Across Looking Like a Baby? What Can I Do To Take The Pain Away?

judge how he should handle himself.

Role Play – Setting parameters are great, but also try role-playing—it's effective. There is a high probability that your son will be offered drugs and or alcohol at some point. You have to give him enough ways to say 'No' and teach him how to handle these awkward discussions with those who might be offering. The best response I have heard that a kid can give a friend trying to get them to indulge is, "I want to have a good time. How can I do that if I am not really aware of what's going on? No thanks!" If your parameters and role-playing fall on deaf ears; I say try the 'scared straight' approach.

As he gets older, visiting a drug rehabilitation center or meeting people (the younger the better) whose lives were affected by substance abuse, might be a good idea. This will give your son a real-life perspective of where this lifestyle will lead.

Violence

Choices: I Am Angry and I Want to Take My Anger Out on Someone

Thoughts for Discussion

Boys commonly engage in horseplay and sometimes through competitiveness it can become very physical or even violent. If you notice that this happens with your son often or he is overly aggressive, it has to be addressed. If your son's behavior becomes physically, verbally, and/or mentally aggressive toward you, another person, or their property, you might be forced to have someone intervene. I would hope in these types of instances his father would be available to help. If he is not available, I recommend that you seek professionals that can assist in identifying what may be at the root of your son's aggressiveness and violence.

If you don't believe intervention is needed and you think your son just needs to blow off steam, get him involved in some type of physical activity. Football, basketball and wrestling are all examples of sports that require a lot of physical activity and will also allow him to work off a little aggression. Make sure you are there for him if he needs to talk, but also getting out a little aggression on a field would be good for him too.

He's Being Targeted by a Bully – Boys that exhibit aggressive behavior, is one thing, but being the target of the aggressive behavior is another. Often times you can determine if your son is the target of a bully if he becomes withdrawn or if his grades slip for no reason. Hopefully you don't have this as a worry, but children are victimizing an alarming number of their peers in a number of ways—the schoolyard bully has evolved.

Students are gaining access to cell phones and social networking sites earlier and earlier and a new form of violence has replaced fighting in many communities – cyber bullying. Schools have begun to take an extremely hard stance against "bullying," whether real or virtual. If you think your son is being targeted, make sure you discuss the situation with him and work together on possible solutions. In some cases, alerting the school or other authorities could make the problem worse. However use your best judgment to determine if you need intervention.

Dealing with Law Enforcement

I Was Pulled Over By a Police Officer, What Should I Do?

Thoughts for Discussion

Critical for teenage boys, especially boys of color, is a conversation about how to handle interactions with law enforcement. In some instances, these tips could prevent future run-ins and in the most extreme cases, jail time or worse. When it comes to law enforcement, remember to give your son two rules: 1) silence is golden and 2) be polite. With that said, here are a couple of specific situations that I think warrant you spending time discussing how to handle:

A Normal Traffic Stop – Reinforce to him the importance of quickly pulling over and offering identification and proper registration. If the stop is at night, turn the interior lights on as well. After that, it is best to remain quiet. If the officer says that your son was speeding, ran a red light or has a tail light missing and he doesn't agree, it doesn't matter. He should be apologetic and move on. Doing this won't affect his ability to fight the ticket later.

I don't want to generalize about law enforcement, so I will speak from my own experiences. I have been pulled over a few times and for the most part the police officers have been extremely professional— we handled our business and I moved on. However I do recall when I was much younger, I would get detained and I felt as if I was being tested to see if I would lose my cool. They would keep me on the side of the road for an inordinate amount of time, make me get out of the car, ask me all kinds of irrelevant questions, just to eventually let me go—without a ticket or explanation. Luckily I never lost my composure, but I know guys that did and it didn't turn out so well. So make sure he does everyone a favor and if in doubt, he should remember to go back to rules one and two.

Also if your son is old enough to drive a car, he has to make sure all lights are operational and he has all forms of current identification-- insurance, and registration—and absolutely no phones, no texting, and always wear a seatbelt.

Request to Search Property – If a police officer makes a request to search your son or his personal property (including his car), I would

Dealing with Law Enforcement

I Was Pulled Over By a Police Officer, What Should I Do?

say no. Again, if he is driving and stopped by the police, he should quickly pull over, turn the interior lights on and have all of his identification ready and available. While you can technically refuse the search under the 4th Amendment; it can be overcome fairly easily. If your son turns the light on to show he has nothing to hide and remains polite, in most cases the police won't take the request further.

This is also the case if your son is the passenger in someone else's car. Again, he should be polite and say as little as possible.

....

Learning to make good decisions makes a difference. I would conclude that a significant portion of the boys that are caught up in the criminal justice system are there because at some point they didn't make good choices. Additionally, the sheer number of children being raised without the benefit of a father points to the fact that, too many men aren't making good choices and certainly aren't taking responsibility for their choices. For this reason, it is extremely important that you identify strategies your son can use to support the goal of making thoughtful decisions.

Priority 3

Pursue Every Opportunity Proactively

"The ladder of success is best climbed by stepping on the rungs of opportunity."

Ayn Rand

Just as she could hunt out a bargain on shoes, with my uncle's help, my mother knew when opportunities or programs and services were available that could benefit my brothers and me. I have to admit that I was probably the biggest benefactor of this. I think I have always been a pretty open-minded person, so I seemed more often than not the one willing to try just about every program or experience. Whether it was a result of being the middle child or not, I benefitted greatly by being receptive. Through these experiences I became involved in Upward Bound, I engaged in recreational sports and I was able to work with some of the best drum instructors in the city. Because of these experiences, I know well the benefits of being receptive to new opportunities and I want to express the importance of encouraging or even insisting that your son try new things even if he doesn't want to. Also through my uncle, I was exposed to the power of mentoring and began a practice of involving my supporters in many aspects of my life.

The opportunities I mentioned were specific to my situation. However there are also opportunities inherent in everyday things we may take for granted, for example, the educational system, tried and true ideas and concepts, and resources specifically designed to support individuals who are trying to help themselves. When I think about the types of resources my family, was able to take advantage of, even in the late 70's and early 80's, it is pretty incredible. One situation that comes to mind is when my youngest brother was born several weeks premature. As a consequence of his early arrival, health problems plagued him early on. I recall my mother having to make endless calls to healthcare professionals, government agencies and schools to ensure he received the special attention he needed. Things weren't always easy to find and the information certainly wasn't centralized, but she made it work. I kept that experience in mind as well as the significance of mentoring to my life, when deciding what types of opportunities were most important to cover in this Priority.

In Chapter 9, I wanted to bring over 100 resources together to support your parenting efforts. However the chapter begins with a detailed look at the different types of mentors and mentoring programs and the value they can bring to your son's life. The additional resources range from educational services and support for a variety of needs to legal and child advocacy assistance. In the first two chapters, I focused on education and finances and why it is important to proactively approach the way in which you manage both of them. Before we get to any of the resources, I wanted to talk about education. I believe education is supremely important because a great education can change the course of a person's life. *In Chapter 7, I focused on the steps you can take to get the most from your son's education and instill a love of learning. In Chapter 8, I've highlighted 6 basic financial concepts and discuss the best way to incorporate them into your families' financial picture.* By doing so, you will be able to run your families finances with more success and long-term efficiency and be in a position to impart these strategies on your son, for his own lifetime of financial health.

Chapter 7

Make the Most of His Educational Experience

Highlights
"Education will most likely serve as the foundation for all your son's future pursuits,—make the most of it."

– Teaming with His Teachers	– Establish Good Study Habits
– Encourage Reading	– Reward Good Performance and Address Low Performance

The value of education cannot be overstated. The ability to read, write, become proficient at math concepts, and learn basic problem-solving techniques, begins in school. In addition, the social dynamics in a traditional academic setting are invaluable to the emotional and social development of your son. Granted, in far too many communities the school systems fall short of what they should be. Whether or not this is your dilemma, the current educational system with its flaws, will most likely serve as the foundation for all your son's future pursuits. For that reason, I suggest that you remember to approach this in a way that will help your son get the most from the experience and foster a life-long love of learning.

If the public schools in your area are not meeting your needs, consider sending your son to a charter or private school or even possibly home schooling him is an option. The key is to identify what educational opportunities are available and pursue them. Private or parochial schools can be costly; however, there is a significant amount of tuition assistance that is available for students—and they are not all needs-based. As for public schools, even those that aren't optimal, if you are willing to work with them, in most cases you will be surprised by the results you get.

As a single mother, you may be facing a widely held belief that, especially among education professionals, you don't get as involved in the educational process. I think it is unfair to generalize, but what the statistics do bear out is that children, boys in particular, raised by single mothers perform 20% worse and have a significantly higher drop-out rate than children raised in two-parent homes. If you are not already engaged in the process or you are engaged but feel you aren't getting the results you desire, there are some basic areas on which you can focus to make the most of his education at school and at home. *Help shape your son's educational experience by establishing a relationship with his teachers, encouraging a love of reading, helping him to develop good study habits, and employing strategies to reward good performance and address low performance in school.*

Teaming with His Teachers

There are a couple of things you can do to gain a better relationship with your son's teachers. First, meet his teachers early in the year before your son gets into the evaluation phase. Share with his teachers your expectations and what you perceive his strengths are as well as his opportunities for growth. It is also important that you communicate things about his personality that will support her effort to educate him. Doing this will help you to establish a rapport with his teachers at the outset and you will be more likely to form a teaming relationship with them. Teachers typically respond positively when they know parents are engaged and supportive. Another thing you can do is request that the teachers help by giving you a signal (for example, an email or note) when your son begins to perform poorly or has recurring behavioral issues. I have found that if you can give immediate attention to problem areas, you have a greater chance of correcting them. If these are issues, the earlier you can diagnose your son's situation the sooner you can determine if there are contributing factors or if additional support is needed.

Encourage Reading

The value of you nurturing a love of reading in your son is immeasurable. Reading is the best, least expensive way to expose your son to life outside his world. Because it is well documented that boys don't read at the same rates or with the same intensity as girls; that is all the more reason to encourage it. Some authors are making the extra effort to write books that will appeal to boys. A list of recommended books, are included in Chapter 9, *100+ Resources*. Periodically I will also feature new books I think young men will find interesting, on my website. For more information on featured books and other information of interest to you and your son, go to: www.1021leadership.org. Aside from finding titles of interest to him, two things you can do to nurture his love of reading are to take frequent trips to the library, especially when he is young, and secondly, let him see you reading books as well. A good idea to help make the most of your combined reading effort is to set aside some time to discuss the books you each are reading.

Establish Good Study Habits

Good study habits can make the difference between your son consistently achieving good marks and not. There are no special provisions needed to make this happen. I suggest that you set aside a regular, daily study time for homework in a quiet, well-lit room. Encourage your son to keep the study area neat and well organized. As your son gets older and assignments get harder, he will have established good habits early on. Remember good grades should be thought of as the by-product of intelligence, good teaching, and good study habits.

Reward Good Performance and Address Low Performance

Your son's good performance in educational endeavors should be acknowledged. When you make a big deal about an accomplishment or academic achievement, he will want to continue the behavior. You will make the final decision, but I don't believe we should get in the habit of giving money for this type of accomplishment because achieving good grades is a result of his investment in his future—it is a baseline expectation that he does his best in academics. If you feel it really important to give tangible gifts, consider making his favorite meal or give him a break from his responsibility to do a chore for one week. When we don't over-gift it is much easier for boys to become self-motivated. Alternatively, if your son is struggling in a particular subject and shows improvement, going above and beyond with studying and completing extra credit assignments; I believe this effort should be rewarded in a more tangible way.

Correcting low performance is not as easy as rewarding good performance, but necessary for obvious reasons. If you have a low performing child, first diagnose the situation. There will be a number of reasons why a child under-performs. Is the problem due to a lack of ability or is it his willingness to do the required work? If he lacks the ability to perform the task, your strategy will be focused on correcting any knowledge deficits or identifying if other problems are at play. If the nature of his issue is developmental, consult the appropriate school personnel to determine the best course of action to get him additional support. I will caution against you allowing the school to label your son as 'special ed.' The statistics that have been shared with me, could lead one to believe that schools may be using this label as an excuse not to teach. I understand that teachers are under incredible pressure to ensure that specific curriculum is taught and taking additional time with one child is almost out of the question. So unless you truly think the label applies, I suggest that you exhaust all resources before you take that path. If developmental issues aren't the problem, I would recommend that you try helping him improve his study habits, solicit help from tutors, and/or request that he spend additional time with his teacher.

If your son lacks motivation or is unwilling to perform, try and understand why your son is unmotivated. Rule out any issues related to home life. Is he bored? Is he over-scheduled? When you do your best to eliminate issues at home, talk to the school's counselor and ask; a) What can be done to challenge your son more?, or b) Does he need to move to a different class? c) Could it be a personality conflict with a teacher or schoolmate? Once you uncover or rule out these issues, be understanding, but he must recognize that your patience will have a limit. Ultimately he is responsible for putting in the necessary effort.

. . . .

Education is the most powerful weapon that can be used to change your life and change the world. Taking proactive steps with the strategies offered in this chapter will support your son's educational pursuits, and will serve him well for the rest of his life. Getting an education is not a luxury, it is a necessity. Make sure you are poised and prepared to help your son make the most of his.

Chapter 8

Encourage a Disciplined Attitude Toward Money

Highlights
"If a person gets his attitude toward money straight, it will help improve almost every other area in his life."

– Establish a Budget and Stick with It	– Protect Your Credit Rating
– Identify and Save for Financial Goals	– Know the Difference Between Assets and Liabilities
– Don't Work Against Your Self Interest	– The Power of Giving

"If a person gets his attitude toward money straight, it will help improve almost every other area in his life." I can attest to that statement. As a result of my earliest experiences with money, my attitude was negatively impacted in ways that I was unaware of until it was almost too late. I believed that financial health meant that "I only needed to have access to cash." In my early professional life, I always had access to money, but never seemed to have financial stability. What I failed to really understand was that unless you can physically print your own money, that kind of thinking would not yield long-term success. Even after I started a family, I still had that attitude, but I started to employ good strategies too; contributing to my 401K, and saving to purchase a home. My wife and I had started to save; we were working and living a reasonable lifestyle, but financially we still weren't getting ahead. I couldn't figure it out then, but now I know it had everything to do with the attitudes I formed early on. Unfortunately it didn't change until we were actually facing bankruptcy. After a few bad financial decisions linked to the pursuit of gaining more money, we looked up and had amassed almost $100,000 in credit card and other unsecured debt. We had just moved to the Northeast and my wife was facing a layoff. We knew things had to change and slowly began to take down the debt. I finally started to understand that in order to better manage our finances and get ahead, I had to get my attitude right. To help drive this point home; my attitude was probably not much different than individuals you hear about who win the lottery and spend it all, or professional athletes and entertainers who go from rags to riches and back to rags again. My highs and lows were not that extreme, but the same mentality is most likely at the root of both.

Another negative behavior that results from this type of attitude is becoming miserly—or downright 'cheap.' Not to be confused with being frugal or spending wisely. Miserly individuals are simply overzealous about not spending money. When an individual refuses to spend or fails to take on a spirit of generosity; he will cut off the flow of money and positive energy into his own life. That may seem a little meta-physical, but a couple of old sayings make the point best, "in life you have to spend money to make money," and "you get what you pay for." While they may be more popular as business mantras, the wisdom of the statements can be applied to your personal finances. I'm not suggesting you spend money for the sake of spending. However I do feel there is value in investing wisely and letting your money work for you. I've seen individuals with this miserly behavior neglect themselves, their property and seem to always take the least expensive way out. Individuals with this mindset don't seem to look at the full picture of value—they are primarily driven by the desire not to spend. At the end of the day, you have to maintain a balanced perspective about your money. Extremes, whether spending too much or too little, will not work long-term.

Once I became aware of the detriment of my attitude and was able to get passed it, I had to begin to consistently use the tried and true concepts about finances that most of us intuitively know but don't always possess the discpline to follow—*establish and stick with a budget, identify and save for financial goals, limit the amount of interest you are paying when possible, protect your credit rating, know the difference between assets and liabilities, and embrace the power of giving.* While my early encounter with finances was not optimal; I recommend that you begin to teach your son about these concepts early. When you approach his financial education proactively and not reactively, it will go a long way in helping to positively shape his attitude about money.

Establish a Budget and Stick with It

Do yourself a huge favor, create a budget specifying how resources, especially money will be allocated or spent during a particular period. I never adhered to budgets, because I thought if I wasn't bound by a budget or left my spending loose I would have more flexibility and control over our financial situation—I was wrong. If you think like this too, I recommend that you take one month and jot down every single thing you spend your money on, that daily cup of coffee, each time you withdraw money out of the accounts without thinking, unplanned grocery shopping trips, etc. You will be amazed at how much money you spend that is completely unaccounted for.

My family did this exercise about 10 years ago and the very next month we created and adhered to our first household budget. Developing a budget is the most important part of smart financial decision-making. In fact, I think of it as a roadmap. You have to have an idea of where you need to go before you can get there—otherwise you are going to be driving all over the place and getting nowhere. The best way to develop this mindset in your son is to let him see you creating and sticking with a household budget for your family. As I am sure you know, a budget helps you to distinguish your 'needs' from your 'wants.' Needs are priorities and have to be budgeted for first. Your wants can be established based on the remaining funds for the month. If you want to start the budgeting process and don't know where to begin or want a centralized place to manage your finances, consider www.mint.com and www.budgettracker.com. These are easy-to-follow online resources you can use to manage your family finances.

A second way to introduce the concept of maintaining a budget to your son is during a shopping trip. When you go shopping, agree on a budget before you start and allow him to make spending decisions based on that predetermined budget. It is a way to impart some knowledge and also keep him pre-occupied.

Identify and Save for Financial Goals

People rarely reach goals they haven't set. Nearly every item your son asks you to purchase for him can become the object of a goal-setting lesson and subsequent opportunity to save his money. Remember the goal of saving money is not just to make an immediate purchase, it also allows you to save for bigger, more important things such as, retirement, college or a rainy day. However what I am suggesting is the easiest way to share the benefits of saving money with your son. As he gets older, you can help him establish longer-term goals that require him to save money over an extended period of time. Once he achieves his goal, he will feel a sense of accomplishment and hopefully appreciate the purchase more. This is also a perfect opportunity to formally establish a savings account for your son at a local bank. When you and your son establish savings accounts with the bank, you will earn a percentage of interest on the money you place in the bank. The more you save, the more opportunity you have to make your money work for you.

Another saving opportunity is through the purchase of stocks and bonds. This certainly is a more complicated concept to explain to your son, but I have identified a company, *Ones Share* that offers an introduction to stock ownership and makes learning about stock ownership fun for a child. To get additional information, go to: www.oneshare.com.

Note: *If you give you son an allowance, encourage saving by giving him his allowance in denominations that follow the strategy just discussed: If you give him $10 a month, do so in increments of 10-one dollar bills and encourage him to set aside $5 dollars for saving.*

Don't Work against Your Self Interest

To keep the concept simple, banks earn money by charging fees and interest—primarily interest on secured loans (home, car or equipment loans), unsecured loans and credit cards. As consumers we have to be careful not to give the money we earned in our savings account (as discussed in the previous section), back to the bank by paying more interest, primarily on credit cards. Credit cards and other types of unsecured debt (any debt that doesn't have a tangible object, like a house or car, connected to it to ensure repayment) is another way financial institutions make money (that means they could be taking yours). The bank charges us interest each day on the balance we carry on our credit cards. Most people carry the balance of their credit card over from month to month and make the minimum payments when due. Unfortunately, when you pay the minimum balance each month, you end up paying much more than the amount the item cost when you first purchased it. The example offered is about Credit Cards, but anytime you pay interest on any type of loan, the sooner you repay the note the better. If that is not an option, paying more than the amount you owe each month, over time helps you reduce the amount of interest you are paying the bank. You could also end up paying the loan off a little earlier. Please know that I understand that cash flow is important and Credit Cards, if kept in perspective, can help you with this. My goal is to remind you of their reality.

Protect Your Credit Rating

As you know, when it comes to finances, we live and die by our 'credit rating.' Explaining a credit rating to your son may be a little cumbersome, but a quick way to describe it is the rating each individual is assigned based on their previous payment history with creditors, how much money they make from work and any unused credit (money) that is available to them. It is extremely important that your son knows a poor credit rating could hinder his ability to make bigger more important purchases like a home for his family or in some cases could even cost him a job. Credit cards are probably the biggest culprit in destroying credit ratings. If your son is going to use credit cards or engage in any type of financial agreement, you have to remind him how important it is to pay his bills on time, every time. Even if he sees you conducting business in the right way, this is one of those rare times when delivering the message is just as important as your actions.

There may be times, when your son simply cannot pay his bills. If that does happen, I am sure you will help him understand that even though he is in a tough spot, he cannot ignore the situation—it won't just go away. Give your creditors a call and make payment arrangements. Financial institutions are actually willing to work with you to find terms that are manageable for everyone.

Know the Difference between Assets and Liabilities

Ask yourself, of the things I own, which ones gain in value or hold their value and which things cost money to own them? Assets gain or appreciate in value or have value, like a house (depending on the situation a home can sit in either column), jewelry, antiques, stocks, bonds, money from work, interest income, etc. Liabilities are things that depreciate or cost money to maintain and offer you little to no value in return or have a reoccurring bill associated with it, for example cars, expensive clothes, utilities, credit cards, rent, etc. It is important that you share with your son that he should hold more assets than liabilities. Making good decisions about big purchases will ultimately determine his financial health. By focusing on assets vs. liabilities, he will be able to make smarter financial decisions.

The Power of Giving

There is an age-old saying that goes "the more you give, the more you receive." There is truth in this statement. Therefore, having a conversation about basic concepts used for financial health would be incomplete without addressing the importance of giving. I am sure that your son can understand the basic benefits of giving; when you help someone in need or give of your time or money your son can learn to have compassion for others. However the reason why I believe the act of giving should be included as a financial concept and not just a 'values' lesson is because when you give of yourself or your resources you truly open the door to receive. Very wealthy people understand this concept well. Not to say that they aren't giving out of the goodness of their hearts, but I tend to think they understand and believe in the reciprocal effect the power of giving has on our lives. There are also tax benefits to giving. Whether you tithe at church or make other donations to charitable organizations, maintain receipts and make the appropriate deductions with your annual income tax return. However, if you are like many individuals; when money is in short supply giving it away may seem ridiculous. It does take faith, but remember money is not the only resource we have at our disposal. We are each blessed with gifts and talents that we can share with others. When we sacrifice by giving of our time or talents it is also a way to inspire the spirit of reciprocity.

. . . .

Financial health is not as much about how much money you make; it's about how much you keep and leverage when needed. Individuals that consistently employ these 6 basic concepts will be in a better position financially. If there was something within the chapter you found helpful and you aren't already doing it, consider implementing it in your family's financial plan. Also, make sure to share these concepts with your son. When he witnesses you managing the family's finances proactively, it will positively impact his attitude about money for the rest of his life.

Chapter 9

Mentoring, Role Models and 100+ Resources

Highlights	
"Don't underestimate the long-term effect that a mentor can have in your son's life. I personally was influenced the most by good men who didn't share my last name."	
– A Mentoring Success Story – Peer Mentors – Role Models	– Leadership Mentoring – 100+ Resources

The most important resource at your disposal is Mentors. Research confirms what we knew anecdotally or intuitively before —that mentoring works. A research brief published by *Child Trends* and titled, "Mentoring: A Promising Strategy for Youth Development," found that youth who participate in mentoring relationships experience a number of positive benefits. Mentored youth perform better in school, are more engaged, have a better chance of going on to higher education, and have better communication skills. Mentored youth also are less likely to abuse drugs, participate in other negative behavior and tend to trust their parents more. In this chapter I will focus on the benefits of mentoring, both traditional and peer mentoring as well as offer you over 100 resources you may find helpful in your role as mother to a growing son. I am a big advocate of engaging mentors because they have been so important to me on my journey. I don't think I have to convince you of the positive impact mentoring can have on your son. Instead I will share two positive stories with you, first my experience with traditional mentors and my experience with a peer mentor. I hope they will fuel your desire to connect your son with a mentor or offer comfort to you that it was the right decision if you have already taken the step. The significance of Role Models is also addressed as well as an introduction to a new approach to mentoring established to provide leadership development and coaching to young men.

A Mentoring Success Story

As I look back at my childhood and think about the people who served as role models and mentors to me, the men that I met through my Uncle Jerry come to mind first. During the summer months, my uncle would send for my brothers and me. During our stays, we met many of his college friends. They offered a unique glimpse of a lifestyle we didn't know existed. My uncle was heavily involved in his fraternity, and he firmly believed that exposure to this organization and the college atmosphere would serve us well later in life. Many of his friends were degreed or pursuing degrees in chemistry, accounting, law, and medicine or were engaged in professions I knew nothing about. It was a very impressionable time in my life and I was intrigued by exposure to the academic and social aspects of college as well as the dynamics of their relationships. Over a span of five years, we came to know my uncle's friends extremely well. To this day we still keep in touch and remain involved in each other's lives. What was most important about my uncle and his friends was their willingness to provide guidance and support to young men they were not related to. When I would report back to them the progress I made over the year or the challenges I faced at critical times in my life, I could sense the pride in their voices when they realized I used information or advice they shared with me to work through a particular situation. These men, role models, mentors, and friends set an exceptional example for my brothers and me, and I've patterned parts of my own life after theirs.

That was my story, but research in both educational settings and in the workplace indicates that students and employees alike are more likely to succeed if they have had a mentor. If you aren't already doing so, I would encourage you to actively engage in discussions with men who can provide support and guidance to your son to achieve his aspirations. I think both formal and informal mentoring relationships are good options. As I explained, most of my mentors were not established in a formal setting. It has been my experience, that there are a number of people willing to serve as mentors, if they are asked. Several national mentoring programs are identified in Chapter 9, 100+ Resources; to get a comprehensive list of local, regional and national mentoring programs, go to: www.mentoring.org. If you and your son are already involved in a mentoring program, keep in mind that successful mentoring is a partnership, where both sides are actively involved. Mentors tend to be successful in most areas of their lives so their time may be limited. Encourage your son to stay flexible for his mentor and stay in touch; it will pay off in the end. Because some, very good men who didn't share my last name personally influenced me the most.

Peer Mentors

Another type of mentoring takes place between peers. This type of mentoring offers another source of support that can help augment a traditional mentoring relationship. Peers tend to relate well with each other because they are typically around the same age and share other common interests. There is a level of comfort that young men have when sharing their views with each other, especially when they have similar interests and trust has been established. I have had the benefit of a few peer mentors and have also had the pleasure of providing guidance and support to many colleagues and friends along the way.

One of my lifelong friends is a perfect example of a positive peer mentor relationship. We met while in college and he has been a constant source of moral support for me. We have many experiences in common. He was also raised by a single mother in Texas. After he finished his college studies, he moved to the Northeast and he has carved out a very successful personal and professional life. It's been helpful to have a friend and mentor who has a similar experience to my own. Many of the situations and challenges I've had along my journey were firsts for me. My friend is a bit older and has always tracked ahead of me with many things related to career, finances, marriage and parenting. He offered an insightful perspective and I adopted some of the strategies he used for dealing with different issues in my life. It is not a stretch to say my peer mentor/friendship has been one of the most significant relationships in my life. I would encourage you to help your son build relationships with his peers, as these relationships may offer another source of guidance and support along his journey. Remember, he may not be able to connect with a lot of peers in this way and it probably won't happen until he matures a bit, but the goal should focus on the quality of his relationships. One great peer mentor is all you need.

Role Models

Just like mentors, having your son identify role models is also an extremely helpful exercise. While some people confuse the two, they serve different purposes. Role models are different from mentors in one very big way: you probably won't have a relationship with your role model. For example, Barack Obama could be your son's role model, but it is unlikely he will have the time to have regularly scheduled meetings with your son. Role models can offer a great example of successful men that have achieved the goals your son sets for himself. When identifying role models, make sure you and your son keeps the following in mind:

Know His Interests – If your son's interests aren't obvious, have a few conversations with him, prod him if necessary to determine what he likes, what subjects in school he prefers, sports he likes to play at recess, etc. Next, have your son identify people that are doing or have done what he likes to do, preferably the "best" people at it. Once he gathers the information you should talk about it. Learn about the person yourself, and show an interest in what they've achieved. Your interest will encourage your son to stay engaged and excited about the person or people he chooses. As he gets older and is prepared to develop a Success Plan (Priority 4, Chapter 11 – Create a Vision and Success Plan for the Future), it will make it easier to identify the role models more closely aligned with the future he sees for himself.

Leadership Mentoring

As a society, we are experiencing a growing leadership void in our families, communities and workforce. I believe we find ourselves in this position because we have become a 'me-first' culture; which has given way to apathy. We have also allowed the media to shape our perceptions of what leadership should look like and in doing so many individuals, specifically the 'average, everyday' guy either doesn't feel equipped to step into the role of leader or he feels he doesn't possess the right credentials or image. The leadership void has existed for a long time, especially in our families and communities. I believe the reason more attention is being paid to it now, is because; first, the enormous numbers of skilled workers (the baby boom generation), who are, or will soon be, leaving the workforce; second, the United States having fallen behind other industrialized nations in almost every metric that determines future growth—has made it clear that we have not laid the ground work to compete or lead in future generations; and finally, with the recent economic downturn, opportunities have greatly diminished yet the requirements for success have increased. These factors have left business leaders around the country scrambling to find answers, without much success. For these reasons, I strongly believe it is important that we create a new blueprint for leadership. A new roadmap—a movement, that will build upon old concepts of what leadership looks like and prepare the next generation, even those individuals considered 'non-traditional,' to compete and succeed in the global economy. In order to make a long-term impact globally we must first start locally—at the family and community level.

When making a determination on how I could help to fill this leadership void, I pulled from my own background for inspiration. As I mentioned, during my journey I have been blessed by having a number of opportunities come my way. What I would consider to be the 3 critical pillars that helped me were, 1) my association with great mentors; 2) growing up I was exposed to a variety of people, places and things outside of my community and; 3) I was able to hone in on something I was naturally good at and stuck with it long enough to develop my natural talents into strengths that I could apply in many areas of my life. I feel strongly that these types of experiences will be extremely helpful to others as well. More importantly, it can serve as a platform to support the development of a new generation of leaders.

To drive this effort, I founded 10.2.1 Leadership (pronounced Ten to One), a non-profit organization established to provide leadership mentoring services to young men. The name Ten to One was chosen to reflect my philosophy that, "No matter what the circumstances, the destiny of 10 or more individuals can be positively impacted when 1 emerges to lead them." Our mission is to work with schools, community organizations and concerned corporations to identify and coach young men that demonstrate the innate leadership qualities and discipline needed to be successful in the program. 10.2.1 is different than traditional mentoring programs; our uniqueness is attributed to the fact that we've developed a project-based curriculum that builds leadership readiness, effective communication and teaming skills. Collectively they represent a critical skillset that will be necessary to navigate our changing world. Additionally, the program serves to foster community involvement and student engagement so that the path to future success becomes clear and within reach. To get more information about what's next for 10.2.1 Leadership, go to www.1021leadership.org.

100+ Resources *

Establishing mentoring relationships is a significant and life-changing opportunity that is available to your son. Yet there are even more options to consider. To get you started on the path to pursing more opportunities, I've identified over 100 resources that offer a variety of programs, information and support that you may find helpful. They have been categorized in a way that identifies what type of support they offer. We will update the list of resources periodically, check out: www.1021leadership.org to get the latest list of national and regional organizations and information that can offer support for you and your son.

Mentoring Programs & Organizations		
Name	**Description**	**Contact Information**
Big Brothers Big Sisters of America	National organization helping men have positive mentoring experiences with children, while at the same time giving back to the community	230 North 13th St. Philadelphia, PA 19107 Phone: 215.567.7000 Fax; 215.567.0394
Boys and Girls Clubs of America	A national organization that seeks to inspire and enable all young people to realize their full potential as productive, responsible, and caring citizens	1275 Peachtree St., NE Atlanta, GA 30309-3506 Phone: 404.487.5700 www.bgca.org
Jumpstart	Jumpstart brings college students and community volunteers together with preschool children in low-income communities for individualized mentoring and tutoring	308 Congress St., 6th Floor Boston, MA 02210 Phone: 617.542.5867 Fax: 617.542.2557 www.readdfortherecord.org
Junior Achievement	National program that teaches children how they can impact the world around them as individuals, workers, and consumers	JA Worldwide 1 Education Way Colorado Springs, CO 80906 Phone: 719.540.8000 Fax: 719.540.6299 www.ja.org
MENTOR/National Mentoring Partnership	MENTOR believes that, with the help and guidance of an adult mentor, each child can	1600 Duke St., Ste 300 Alexandria, VA 22314 Phone: 703.224.2200

Mentoring Programs & Organizations		
Name	**Description**	**Contact Information**
	discover how to unlock his or her potential	www.mentoring.org
National CARES Mentoring Movement	National organization that promotes the mobilization of African Americans to take the lead in fulfilling society's spiritual and social responsibility to children	230 Peachtree St., Ste 530 Atlanta, GA 30303 Phone: 404.584.2744 Fax: 404.525.6226 www.caresmentoring.com
Police Athletic League	National program in which members of the law enforcement community initiates prevention services with youth in the community	34 ½ East 12th St. NY, NY 10003 Toll free: 800.725.4543 Phone: 212.477.9450 Fax: 212.477.4792 www.palnyc.org

Education Support Organizations		
Name	**Description**	**Contact Information**
A Better Chance	A Better Chance is the oldest and only national organization of its kind changing the life trajectory for academically talented youth of color via access to rigorous and prestigious educational	240 West 35th Street, 9th Floor New York, NY 10001-2506 Main Line: (646) 346-1310 Fax: (646) 346-1311 Toll Free CPSP: (800) 562-7865 www.abetterchance.org

Education Support Organizations		
Name	**Description**	**Contact Information**
	opportunities for students in grades 6-12	
Ace Mentor Program of America	National organization that informs high school students of career opportunities in architecture, construction, and engineering, and to provide scholarship opportunities	400 Main St., Ste 600 Stamford, CT 06901 Phone: 203.323.0020 Fax: 203.323.0032 www.acementor.org
Action for Healthy Kids	National organization that is committed to engaging diverse organizations, leaders and volunteers in actions that foster sound nutrition and physical activity in schools	4711 Golf Rd., Ste 625 Skokie, IL 60076 Toll free: 800.416.5136 Fax: 847.329.1849 www.actionforhealthykids. org
Atlas Communities	National organization dedicated to improving student learning by combining innovative learning experiences with state and local standards	249 Glenbrook Rd., Unit 2224 Storrs, CT 06269-2224 Toll free: 888.577.8585 Fax: 860.486.6348 www.atlascommunities.org
Banking on Our Future	National organization that provides on-the ground and online financial literacy programs that teach children basic money skills	Hope Global Headquarters 707 Wilshire Blvd., 30th floor Los Angeles, CA 90017 Toll Free: 877.592.4673 Phone: 213.891.2900 Fax: 213.489.7511

Education Support Organizations		
Name	**Description**	**Contact Information**
		www.bankingonourfuture. org
Brown Bookshelf	Run by a group of writers, the website is committed to keeping you aware of books that are written by African American authors or contain a majority of African American characters	www.thebrownbookshelf. com
Children's Scholarship Fund	The Children's Scholarship Fund aims to maximize educational opportunity for all children: for those in need by offering tuition assistance in grades K-8 for alternatives to faltering conventional schools and for all children by supporting and cultivating education reform and school choice efforts	Children's Scholarship Fund 8 W. 38th Street, 9th Floor New York, NY 10018 Phone: (212) 515-7100 Fax: (212) 515-7111 e-Mail: info@scholarshipfund.org www.scholarshipfund.org
Fuqua Film Program	Twelve-week summer film intensive in Brownsville, Brooklyn (NY area)	511 6th Ave., Ste #35 NY, NY 10011 Phone: 917.494.7209 www.fuquafilmprogram. org
Ghetto Film School, Inc.	Connects talented young people to artistic educational, and career	P.O. Box 1580 Blvd. Station Bronx, NY 10459 Phone: 718.589.5470

Education Support Organizations		
Name	**Description**	**Contact Information**
	opportunities in the world of film and video (NY area)	Fax: 718.589.2204 www.ghettofilm.org
Hip Hop 4 Life	National organization dedicated to empowering young people to adopt healthy lifestyles. Hip Hop 4 Life serves young people ages ten through eighteen, with a special emphasis on at-risk and low-income youth	511 Ave. of Americas NY, NY 10011 Phone: 646.706.7370 Fax: 646.706.7377
Hip-Hop Educational Literacy Program (H.E.L.P)	As a teaching tool, H.E.L.P. promotes literacy, critical analysis, and differentiated instruction while meeting the needs of all types of learners. The creation of H.E.L.P. came out of a desire to use the influence of Hip Hop music on the 21st century student, to strengthen their abilities in reading and writing	www.edlyrics.com
Home School Association	The American Homeschool Association has been serving homeschooling families with advocacy, support, information and networking since 1995. The AHA supports,	www.americanhomeschool association.org

Education Support Organizations		
Name	**Description**	**Contact Information**
	encourages and promotes all approaches to bona fide homeschooling	
Institute for Responsible Citizenship	National organization that prepares high achieving African-American men for successful careers in business, law, government, public service, education, journalism, the sciences, medicine, ministry, and the arts	1227 25th St., NW, 6th floor Washington, DC 20037 Phone: 202.659.2831 Fax: 202.659.0582 www.i4rc.org
Jackie Robinson Foundation	National organization that serves as an advocate for young people with the greatest need and offers an extensive mentoring program and summer internships	1 Hudson Square 75 Varick St., 2nd floor NY, NY 10013 Phone: 212.290.8600 Fax: 212.290.8081 www.jackierobinson.org
Kanye West Foundation	Provides underserved youth access to music product programs that will enable them to unleash their creative ability and reach their full potential (LA area)	8560 West Sunset Blvd., Ste 210 West Hollywood, CA 90069 www.kanyewestfoundation.org
KIPP Schools	National network of free, open enrollment, college-prep public schools with a track	135 Main St., Ste 1700 San Francisco, CA 94105 Toll free: 866.345.KIPP

Education Support Organizations		
Name	**Description**	**Contact Information**
	record of preparing students in underserved communities for success in college and in life	Fax: 415.348.0588 www.kipp.org
National Alliance for Public Charter Schools	National organization that fosters an environment in which parents can be more involved, teachers are given the freedom to innovate, and students are provided the structure they need to learn	1101 15th St., NW, Ste 1010 Washington, DC 20005 Phone: 202.289.2700 Fax: 202.289.4009 www.publiccharters.org
National Institute for Literacy	National organization aims to improve opportunities for adults, youths, and children to thrive in a progressively literate world	1775 I St., NW, Ste 730 Washington, DC 20006 Phone: 202.233.2025 Fax: 202.233.2050 www.nifl.gov
National Urban Technology Center, Inc.	National organization established to provide access to technology and training to address the widening computer literacy and achievement gap in inner-city communities through its two flagship programs, SeedTech and the Youth Leadership Academy (YLA)	80 Maiden Lane, Ste 606 NY, NY 10038 Toll free: 800.998.3212 Fax: 212.528.7355 www.urbantech.org
Operation HOPE	America's first non-profit social investment	Hope Global Headquarters 707 Wilshire Blvd., 30th

Education Support Organizations		
Name	**Description**	**Contact Information**
	bank and a national provider financial literacy and economic empowerment programs free of charge	floor Los Angeles, CA 90017 Toll Free: 877.592.4673 Phone: 213.891.2900 Fax: 213.489.7511 www.operationhope.org
Steve Harvey Foundation	National organization dedicated to improving public schools in urban areas by upgrading facilities and providing educational and mentoring opportunities that enable students to realize their dreams	3495 Piedmont Rd., Bldg 11, Ste 560 Atlanta, GA 30305 www.steveharveyfoundation.com
Tavis Smiley Foundation	National organization that develops young leaders with critical-thinking skills who will share their knowledge and abilities and make a positive impact on the world	4434 Crenshaw Blvd., Los Angeles, CA 90043 Phone: 323.290.1888 Fax: 323.290.1988 www.youthtoleaders.org
The Association for Library Service to Children (ALSC)	The world's largest organization dedicated to the support and enhancement of library service to children	www.ala.org
The Coalition of Educating Boys of Color	National organization that promotes and supports schools determined to make success an attainable goal for all of their male	14 Priscilla Way Lynn, MA 01904 Phone: 781.775.9461 Fax: 781.593.896 www.coseboc.org

Education Support Organizations		
Name	**Description**	**Contact Information**
	students of color	
The Tom Joyner Foundation	National organization committed to helping students continue their education at black colleges	www.blackamericaweb.com
United Negro College Fund (UNCF)	Nation's most comprehensive higher education assistance organization for students of color. UNCF provides scholarships and internships for students, as well as faculty and administrative professional training	8260 Willow Oaks Corporate Dr. P.O. Box 10444 Fairfax, VA 22031 www.uncf.org
WorldofMoney.org (WoM)	National organization focused on improving the financial literacy of underserved youth ages twelve through eighteen through workshops designed to help students become financially responsible	Phone: 212 969.0339 www.worldofmoney.org
One Share	Through their My First Stock product, OneShare intorduces kids of all ages to stock ownership. Stock Matters, guides children through the wide world of stock ownership. Kids will learn about the elements	www.oneshare.com

Education Support Organizations		
Name	**Description**	**Contact Information**
	of a stock certificate, annual meetings, voting, annual reports and dividends. One Share is a commerce site, but the information could prove helpful.	
Young People's Project (YPP)	National organization that uses math literacy as a tool to encourage young leaders to radically change the quality of education and life in their communities	YPP Chicago 3424 South State, Ste IC3-2 Chicago, IL 60616 Phone: 773.407.4732 www.typp.org

Legal Support & Child Advocacy		
Name	Description	Contact Information
Children's Defense Fund (CDF) Freedom Schools	The CDF Freedom Schools program partners with community-based organizations to provide free summer and after-school care that helps children and youths better fulfill their potential	25 E. St., NW Washington, DC 20001 Toll free: 800.CDF.1200 www.childrensdefense.org
Concerned Black Men (CBM)	National organization that provides youth development services to children from disadvantaged communities	Thurgood Marshall Cntr 1816 12th St., NW, Ste 204 Washington, DC 20009 Toll free: 888.395.7816 Phone: 202.783.6119 Fax: 202.783.2480 www.cbmnational.org
Gay, Lesbian and Straight Education Network (GLSEN)	National organization that ensures that every member of the school community is valued and respected regardless of sexual orientation or gender identity/expression	90 Broad St., 2nd Floor NY, NY 10004 Phone: 212.727.0135 Fax: 212.727.0254 www.glsen.org
Generations United	National organization focused on improving the lives of children and older people through intergenerational programs	1331 H St., NW, #900 Washington, DC 20005 Phone: 202.289.3979 Fax: 202.289.3952 www.gu.org
NAACP	NAACP ensures the political, educational, social, and economic equality of rights of all	4805 Mt. Hope Dr. Baltimore, MD 21215 Toll Free: 877.NAACP-98

Legal Support & Child Advocacy		
Name	**Description**	**Contact Information**
		www.naacp.org
National Council of La Raza (NCLR)	National Hispanic civil rights and advocacy organization	Raul Yzaguirre Bldg 1126 16th St., NW Washington, DC 20036 Phone: 202.785.1670 Fax: 202.776.1792 www.nclr.org
National Urban League	In national partnership with the National CARES Mentoring Movement in its attempt to galvanize millions of committed, conscientious and capable mentors to support today's youth	120 Wall St., 8th Floor NY, NY 10005 Phone: 212.558.5300 www.nul.org
Raising Him Alone	The Raising Him Alone Campaign is committed to increasing advocacy for single mothers raising boys	Raising Him Alone/Urban Leadership Institute 2437 Maryland Ave. Baltimore, MD 21218 Toll free: 877.339.4300 www.raisinghimalone.com

Community Service Organizations		
Name	**Description**	**Contact Information**
100 Black Men of America, Inc.	National organization dedicated to improving the quality of life within the black community and enhancing educational and economic opportunities for all African-Americans	www.100blackmen.org
Alpha Phi Alpha	National fraternity committed to the development and mentoring of youth and provides service and advocacy for the African American Community	2313 Saint Paul St. Baltimore, MD 21218 Phone: 410.554.0040 Fax: 410.554.0054 www.alpha-phi-alpha.com
Boys Scouts of America	Boy Scouts provides a program for young people that builds character, trains them in the responsibilities of citizenship, and develops their personal fitness	www.scouting.org
National Alliance of African American Athletes	National organization that serves to empower young men through athletics, education, and public programs	P.O. Box 60743 Harrisburg, PA 17106 Phone: 717.234.6352 Fax: 717.652.3207
The Links, Incorporated	National organization dedicated to mentoring and preparing black children for a bright future	1200 Massachusetts Ave., NW Washington, DC 20005 Phone: 202.842.8686 Fax: 202.842.4020 www.linksinc.org

Community Service Organizations		
Name	**Description**	**Contact Information**
YMCA	With over 2,500 facilities across the nation. They respond to critical social needs by drawing on it's collective strength	YMCA of the USA 101 North Wacker Dr. Chicago, IL 60606 Toll free: 800.872.9622 www.ymca.net
Youth Baseball: Little League Baseball	The mission for the Little League Baseball and Softball and national partner, Positive Coaching Alliance, is to help all Little League players become Triple-Impact Competitors. A Triple-Impact Competitor works as hard as possible to make an impact on three levels: Improving yourself as a player and person, Helping your teammates improve and Improving the sport as a whole	www.littleleague.org
Youth Basketball	Youth Basketball of America strives to provide opportunities for personal growth and development of youth athletes while also reinforcing positive influences, self-confidence, self-esteem and the ability to excel on and off the court	www.yboa.org

Community Service Organizations		
Name	**Description**	**Contact Information**
Youth Basketball: AAU – Amateur Athletic Union	Offers amateur athletes and volunteers opportunities to develop to their highest level through a national and local network of sporting events. Through participation in AAU, members achieve their dreams as athletes and as valued citizens of the community	www.aausports.org
Youth Football: Football University (FBU)	One of a kind football training experience, focusing on developing and training advanced position enhancing the playmaking ability and skill of elite-level athletes in 6th to 12th grade	www.footballuniversity.org
Youth Football: Pop Warner Little Scholars and Youth Football League	Pop Warner is the nation's largest and oldest youth football and youth cheerleading organization with over 425,000 participants in 44 states and six countries	www.popwarner.com

Social Services		
Organization	**Service**	**Contact**
Boys Town	National organization that serves children and their families through its life-changing youth care and health care programs	National Hotline: 800.448.3000 www.boystown.org
Child Support Collections	Includes child support collection laws and state rules to get help collecting child support	www.child-support-collection.com
Children's Health Fund	National organization committed to providing health care to the nation's most medically underserved children	215 West 125th St., Ste 301 NY, NY 10027 Phone: 212.535.9400 www.childrenshealthfund.org
Department of Education	ED's mission is to promote student achievement and preparation for global competitiveness by fostering educational excellence and ensuring equal access	www.ed.gov
Department of Health and Human Services	The United States government's principal agency for protecting the health of all Americans and providing essential human services	www.hhs.gov
Financial Aid	An office of the U.S. Department of Education, ensures that all eligible individuals can benefit from federally funded financial assistance for education beyond high	www.fafsa.ed.gov

Social Services		
Organization	**Service**	**Contact**
	school	
Head Start	Head Start believes that all children should reach their full potential and every child can succeed. We can impact the success of "at risk" children through, quality early education	www.nhsa.org
Planned Parenthood	Planned Parethood Federation of America is the nation's leading sexual and reproductive health care provider and advocate	www.plannedparenthood.org
United Way	We envision a world where all individuals and families achieve their human potential through education, income stability and healthy lives	www.liveunited.org

Books		
Book Title/Author	**Overview**	**Age**
Bat Boy and His Violin E.B. Lewis	Reginald loves to create beautiful music on his violin. But Papa, manager of the Dukes, the worst team in the Negro National League, needs a bat boy, not a 'fiddler,' and traveling with the Dukes doesn't leave Reginald much time for practicing. Soon he finds an answer for all that	Young Reader
Bronx Masquerade Nikki Grimes	When Wesley Boone writes a poem for his high school English class and reads it aloud, poetry-slam-style, he kicks off a revolution	Teen Reader
Brothers of the Knight Debbi Allen	Reverend Knight can't understand why his twelve sons' sneakers are torn to threads each and every morning, and the boys aren't talking. They know their father would surely put an end to their all-night dance parties. Maybe Sunday, a pretty new nanny can get to the bottom of it	Young Reader
Do I Have a Daddy? Jean neWarren & Warren Lindsay	Thousands of children are forced to grow up without their fathers. This book helps kids with absent, deceased, and unknown dads talk about and deal with this difficult situation	Young Reader
Holding Her Head High: Janine Turner	Single moms are not just a product of our modern culture. There have been single mothers throughout history, women who have raised not only their children but also nations with a higher vision for life. *Holding Her Head High* recounts stories of twelve such women from the third to the twenty-first centuries, women who found ways to twist their fates to represent God's destiny for their lives	Adult
I Can't Accept Not Trying: Michael Jordan	Michael Jordan's success as a basketball player didn't happen by accident. In *I Can't Accept Not Trying*, Jordan writes about the simple truths behind his self-discipline and passion for personal excellence	All Ages

Books		
Book Title/Author	**Overview**	**Age**
Ma Dear's Aprons Patricia McKissack	A moving portrait of what life was like in the turn-of-the-century South for a poor single mother and her son in a time before washing machines, cars, and TV sets. Monday means washing, with Ma Dear scrubbing at her rub board in her blue apron. Tuesday is ironing, in a sunshine-yellow apron that brightens Ma Dear's spirits. And so it goes a different chore and a different apron for every day of the week. But come Sunday, the sweet reward is a picnic by the creek -- mother and son alone together with nothing to do but enjoy each other's company	Young Reader
Magic Treehouse Series Mary Pope Osborne	When they are in the tree house, Jack and Annie only have to say those simple words and the tree house starts to spin, faster and faster. . . . And then, *poof!*—the kids find themselves flying on the backs of dinosaurs, exploring the surface of the moon, and slipping down the deck of the *Titanic*	Young Reader
No Excuses! Dr. Wayne Dyer	Topic of 'excuses' and how they can do more harm than we realize. The book demonstrates how excuses go far beyond "my dog ate my homework," and can actually become words that prevent your child from reaching his or her potential	Young Reader
Oh, the Places You'll Go Dr. Seuss	"Don't be fooled by the title of this seriocomic ode to success; it's not 'Climb Every Mountain,' kid version. All journeys face perils, whether from indecision, from loneliness, or worst of all, from too much waiting	All Ages

Books		
Book Title/Author	**Overview**	**Age**
Outliers:Tthe Story of Success Malcolm Gladwell	In this stunning new book, Malcolm Gladwell takes us on an intellectual journey through the world of "outliers"—the best and the brightest, the most famous and the most successful. He asks the question: what makes high-achievers different? His answer is that we pay too much attention to what successful people are like, and too little attention to where they are from: that is, their culture, their family, their generation, and the idiosyncratic experiences of their upbringing. Along the way he explains the secrets of the successful	Adult
Percy Jackson and they Olympians Series Rick Riordan	Humans and half-bloods alike agree—Percy Jackson and the Olympians is a series fit for heroes! Re-live the adventure from the beginning with this boxed set of the first three books	Teen Readers
Raising You Alone Warren Hanson	This is an essential book for any single-parent family. With heart and humor, it talks about the quirks and challenges that must be faced every day. A picture book for parents as well as children, this honest, engaging story is the perfect way to say, "I will always love you."	Adults
Salt in His Shoes: Michael Jordan in Pursuit of a Dream Deloris Jordan	As a child, Michael almost gave up on his hoop dreams, all because he feared he'd never grow tall enough to play the game that would one day make him famous. That's when his mother and father stepped in and shared the invaluable lesson of what really goes into the making of a champion — patience, determination, and hard work	Young Reader
Taking Sides Gary Soto	Lincoln Mendoza has to face his homeboys when his posh new school goes up against his old school on the basketball court	Teen Reader

Books		
Book Title/Author	**Overview**	**Age**
We Beat the Street Sharon Draper	Growing up on the rough streets of Newark, New Jersey, Rameck, George, and Sampson could easily have followed their childhood friends into drug dealing, gangs, and prison. But when a presentation at their school made the three boys aware of the opportunities available to them in the medical and dental professions, they made a pact among themselves that they would become doctors	Teen Reader and Adult
Ziggy and the Black Dinosaurs Book Series Sharon Draper	Ziggy, Rashawn, Jerome, and Rico -- the Black Dinosaurs -- are thrilled to discover that their hometown was a stop on the Underground Railroad. Even more exciting, their new friend Mr. Greene has given them an old map that shows a secret passage, dating back to the days of the Railroad, right under their own school!	Young Reader

Websites	
URL	**Overview**
Parenting	
www.boysread.org	An organization of parents, educators, librarians, mentors, authors, and booksellers. Our mission is to transform boys into lifelong readers
www.budgettracker.com	Offers information to help you start the budgeting process when you don't know where to begin or if you want a centralized place to manage your finances
www.couponmom.com	Offers free printable coupons
www.coupons.com	Offers grocery coupons, recipe coupons and internet coupons
www.education.com	Provides parents of school-aged children with free access to information and resources to give them the answers they need - plus activities and articles that make learning together more fun for everyone
www.helpsinglemomsnow. com	Many organizations around the world have taken action towards providing assistance for single moms who are in need. This is fortunate for the single mothers of today, as it is much easier to get help as a single mom in all sorts of different ways. All that is left, then, is to know where to start your search and how to look for such aids
www.juniormagazine.com	Junior is a magazine dedicated to supporting educators and parents for boys ages 9-19
www.mint.com	If you want to start the budgeting process and don't know where to begin or want a centralized place to manage your finances
www.oneshare.com	One Share offers an introduction to stock ownership that is easy to understand and

Websites	
URL	**Overview**
	fun for children
www.singlemommyhood. com	Advice and content for single moms and single dads. Moms and dads talk to us first. The new distination for singlemommyhood
www.smartsource.com	Coupons, Online Coupons - Coupons.SmartSource.com. Free coupons and discounts for top brands
www.weparent.com	A Georgia based network for single parents, co-parents and blended families seeking resources to support positive parenting
Kid-Friendly	
www.addictinggames.com	Play over 3000 free online games! Including arcade games, puzzle games, funny games, sports games, shooting games, and more
www.chess4kids.com	Teaches children to play and win at chess. It contains many interactive chess exercises in a child friendly online web interface
www.funbrain.com	The #1 site for online educational games for kids of all ages. (math, grammar, science, spelling, history)
www.jamstudio.com	Create music beats - free online music mixing & songwriting tool - quickly create backing tracks, karaoke songs, soundtracks & demo songs with professional sounds. JamStudio is perfect for songwriters, musicians, producers or any music enthusiast
www.kbears.com	Interactive Flash website for young children includes educational activities as well as fun and games
www.kid.discovery.com	Discovery Kids inspires kids to explore the awesome world around them and satisfy their curiosity with innovative games,

Websites	
URL	**Overview**
	activities, quizzes and articles
www.kids.gov	The U.S. government's portal site that provides a gateway to hundreds of Federal and other websites for use by kids and teens
www.kids.nationalgeo graphic.com	Features different people, animals, and places each month with facts, games, activities, and related links
www.nflrush.com	The official NFL site for kids. Your source for fun NFL online games, contests, fantasy football, youth football, and NFL Play 60
www.nick.com	Play kids games, watch video from popular kid's shows, play free online games for kids, & more at Nick.com, Nickelodeon's online place for Kids!
www.pbskids.org	Play educational games, watch PBS KIDS shows and find activities like coloring and music. PBS KIDS Games and Shows are research based and vetted by experts
www.sikids.com	Sports news, games, cartoons, and fantasy leagues, specifically designed for kids
www.timeforkids.com	The latest news from around the world for kids in grades K-6. Includes related polls, games, and websites

* Please Note – The <u>100+ Resources</u> chapter, does not represent an endorsement of any of these organizations or websites. The list has been collected to demonstrate the types of support that are available to assist you with your parenting responsibilities. Additionally, it is recommended that you review the kid-friendly websites first to establish your own comfort level.

....

As a single mother you are tasked with many roles and responsibilities, why not make the burden lighter by taking advantage of opportunities that already are within reach. As we discussed in the chapter, the most important resource you can use to support your effort to raise a successful son, are mentors. Mentoring is no longer one-size fits all. You can identify mentors that are specific to your son interests, peer mentors, leadership mentors, virtual mentors, etc. The trick is to engage them early and as often as you can. Additionally, I am leaving you with a list of over 100 helpful resources that can support what you are trying to achieve with your son—all you have to do is reach out.

Priority 4

Envision a Path to Success

"The world makes a way for the man who knows where he is going."

Ralph Waldo Emerson

Growing up, I was told to work really hard and success would happen for me. Somehow I always felt those words were filled with an empty promise. Nevertheless, I did just that as it seemed to be the best approach I'd heard. As I grew through my teen years and into college; all that hard work seemed like a ball & chain tied to my ankle. It didn't sink in until I was much older that I had spent most of my life and energy working hard and not necessarily smart. Primarily because I was working hard to avoid a lifestyle that I didn't want instead of knowing and pursing the life I wanted. I would estimate that it cost me about 15 years of the life God intended for me, because I failed to have a plan early on. One may take the position that, in life things happen when they are supposed to. I tend to disagree as it relates to pursuing goals, because I have seen it time and time again; so many people miss out on opportunities because they simply aren't prepared for them.

When you have an idea of what you want to do and a clear plan for pursuing it, you are more likely to be in a position to recognize opportunities that are related to your goals and will have prepared yourself to take advantage of them as they come. I count myself blessed because of the shear number of opportunities that came my way. I was ready for some of them and others I was not. In any event, I tried to make the best of each situation and didn't fault anyone for my lack of preparation. However, I now know that there are a few more requirements for success than simply working hard. With the understanding that hard work is just a component of success; another, more critical component is the need to create an intentional plan and path for success.

In Priorities 1 – 3, I outlined a systematic approach that helps your son establish a solid foundation for his long-term success. In Priority 4, I will build on that foundation with actionable steps you and your son can take to identify what he would like to do with his life and develop a plan for getting there. *The significance of identifying your son's natural talents will be discussed in Chapter 10. When you know what his talents are and can describe them in a way that is relevant to him, it will serve as the basis for outlining how he can achieve his long-term goals. In Chapter 11, a Success Planning process is presented so that you can uncover his future endeavors with the creation of a vision statement and a plan to prioritize the steps needed to realize the vision. Once your son's plan is developed, he has to be prepared to make it happen. In Chapter 12, to elaborate, I identified*

3 characteristics that I believe all successful men engage when they are in pursuit of their highest goals. Whether they employ them individually or collectively, successful men make things happen by being–Ready, Relentless and Resilient. Successful men are prepared and Ready to meet the challenges they face in life, they demonstrate a Resilient spirit in the face of obstacles and let downs, and most important, successful men Relentlessly pursue their vision with an "at-all-cost," mentality.

Chapter 10

Play to His Strengths

Highlights
"Innate in all of us is the desire to feel that, just as we are, we possess something about us that is unique, relevant, and valuable."

– Strengths-based Approach	– Options for His Future

As a mother, you are your son's best advocate. You play a critical role in helping him see and focus on the best in himself. To prepare your son for the journey to adulthood, one of the most important things you can do is identify and celebrate his natural talents. These are the assets with which he was born; and with these talents, he will be able to make a meaningful contribution to society.

Most adults who are leading worthwhile lives are doing so by mobilizing the natural talents they have honed over time. As a manager of people, I've had the opportunity to read several books about this concept and the process of Strengths-based Management. In the past, I used many of the strategies with my teams and received very positive results. Actually, I was so impressed with the results that I implemented some of the same ones with my own family and saw similar positive results. When I began contemplating the next chapter of my life, I decided that a mentoring/leadership development program was the way to go, and having a strengths-based approach as a part of it was an absolute must. Once I made the decision to proceed, I became a Certified Strengths Advocate through the Gallup organization's Clifton School, and soon after established *The 10.2.1 Project*, a leadership mentoring program that I introduced in the previous chapter. *While there is a sytematic approach to the Strengths-based philosophy, we won't be covering it in its entirety within this* *book. H*owever, what I will do in this chapter is to provide some insight into using your strengths that you will hopefully get excited about employing the approach with your son.

Innate in all of us is the desire to feel that, just as we are, we possess something about us that is unique, relevant, and valuable. Through 30 years of research the Gallup organization identified and documented groundbreaking findings that changed the way we should think about ourselves. Gallup, a leader in the strengths-based approach, found that individuals that can identify their existing talents, give a name to them and understand what they can do to leverage them to more effectively manage their lives today and in the future were motivated, contributed to higher self esteem and offered them a renewed sense of hope. Most of the individuals involved in the research, up to that point, rarely identified themselves in positive terms. Not to suggest that most of these individuals were hopeless, but as a society we often focus on improving our shortcomings, not looking at what we already do well in order to cope and compete in our lives. Most of us spend our lives trying to improve what people perceive as our weaknesses.

When your son focuses on mastering things that are unnatural to him, he could begin to feel like a right-handed person forced to always use his left hand. He can still write his name, but he would do a much better job if he used the hand to which writing comes naturally. This focus on improving weaknesses keeps most people feeling as if they don't measure up. I am not suggesting that you shouldn't seek to improve your son or yourself for that matter, we all should. Seeking to improve the way we write, by learning how to write more eloquently or succinctly is a more realistic goal. For many of our boys, particularly at-risk boys, labels are placed on them by others and unfortunately, some of these labels are not very positive. This may come as no surprise to you, but you may find that there are some people around your son who would prefer to see his weaknesses and will want to label him and his behavior in less-than-positive ways. These labels can shape how boys view themselves. Having a positive self-label, regarding things he does well will naturally help build the foundation for a healthy level of self-respect.

The Strengths-based Approach

The Strengths-based approach has a set of key terms that serve four distinctly different purposes—Talents, Strengths, Skills, and Knowledge. **Talents** are those God-given traits or characteristics people would say come naturally to you. **Strengths** can be developed when we learn and use specific skills and/or knowledge to enliven our natural talents. **Skills** are basic abilities that are learned, and allow you to perform specific steps to a task. Typically skills aren't innate, but it could be that a particular skill-set could certainly come easily to you. An example of a skill is, knowing how to operate a computer. **Knowledge** is not innate, but is a learned process or concept. An individual can acquire knowledge for example, when you learn how to write a computer program, you have gained knowledge. A visual depiction how your natural talents are fortified by the skills and activities you acquire appears in Figure 2.

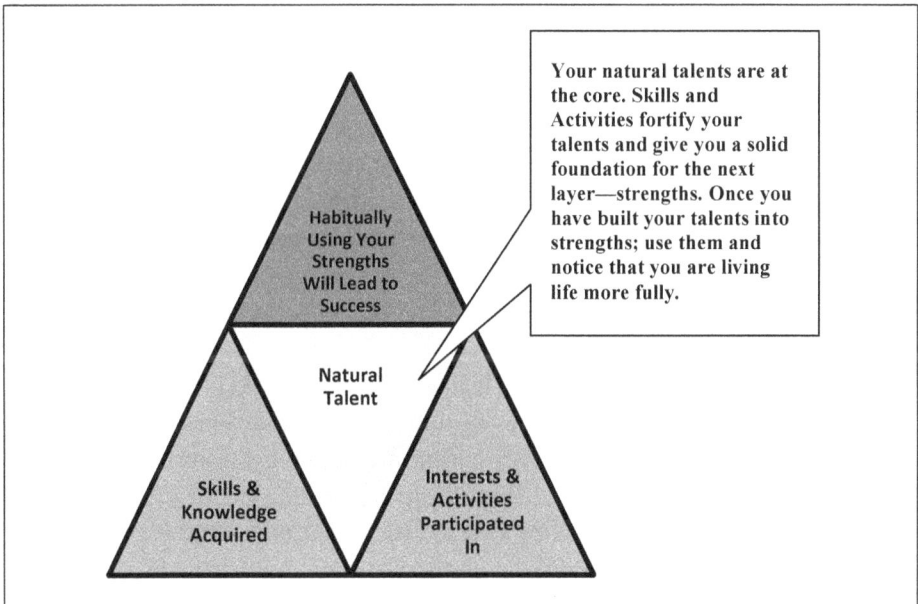

Your natural talents are at the core. Skills and Activities fortify your talents and give you a solid foundation for the next layer—strengths. Once you have built your talents into strengths; use them and notice that you are living life more fully.

Habitually Using Your Strengths Will Lead to Success

Natural Talent

Skills & Knowledge Acquired

Interests & Activities Participated In

Figure 2: Strength Progression Pyramid

As for my own personal journey of discovery; some things were confirmed for me when I first went through an assessment with my team earlier in my career. However, I learned even more about my talents during the process of becoming a Certified Strengths Advocate. One specific talent identified as part of my assessment was a talent equivalent to 'Caring,' as identified in the Talent Names Figure 3. During my career in sales I learned the skill of overcoming objections as well as several techniques designed to close the sale. When I apply my natural talent of 'caring' with these skills, along with the knowledge I gain about the client during the selling process, in most situations, I am able to achieve much higher close rates than my colleagues. My selling success has always been noticeably linked back to client satisfaction and the fact that clients for the most part reported that, while they knew I was interested in closing the deal, they felt as if I was just as concerned with ensuring that their needs were met in the process. During my career, I've been fortunate to consistently take-over low-performing markets and see anywhere from 100% to 200% improvement as a result of using this approach to establish relationships with clients. Throughout this experience I also realized, that the most satisfying times in my life came when I was able to use my talents on a regular basis.

So imagine being able to describe or put a name on a positive attribute you see in your son. For example, do you find that your son is naturally comfortable acting or speaking in front of others, or when he is working in a group or team, does he naturally assume leadership positions and do others trust him enough to follow him? He could have the talent of 'charismatic.' Or consider this, does he have a natural curiosity, ask lots of questions, like to solve mysteries or put puzzles together? He could possess the talent of a 'curious' individual.

My mother would be the first to say that I have always been a compassionate person and try to understand the views of others. However, neither she nor I ever thought that being compassionate or 'caring,' was an actual talent that could be leveraged in order to help me become successful in other ways. This point is critical because it is important for you to be vigilant about noticing recurring or prevalent personality traits; these characteristics more than likely will fall into the category of a natural talent. While it is a good idea to have a formal strength-assessment for your son; you can complete the steps in the next two chapters, without doing so.

Human beings are so complex and multifaceted we could have a variety of talents. You can make the observation as mentioned and use one or more of the names identified in Figure 4 to determine your son's talents. I have offered a general description of typical talents children possess. What is most important in this exercise is that you recognize when your son frequently displays certain behaviors, similar to those listed.

Talent Name	General Description
Accomplish	Likes to complete or achieve goals
Caring	Showing concern and compassion for others
Competitor	Desire to win or engage in activites against others to show dominance
Assured	Confident about personal abilities or qualities
Reliable	Trustworthy and able to do what is expected or has been promised
Curious	Eager to know about something, someone or how to manipulate it
Visionary	Idealistic, and having foresight about a variety of things
Arranger	Likes to organize or put people or things in order
Charismatic	Possessing great powers of charm or influence
Communicate	Have the ability to reveal thoughts, feelings verbally or in writing

Figure 3: Talent Names, Defined by *10.2.1 Leadership*

Once you have identified 2 or more Talent Names, help your son determine what types of skills and knowledge he can acquire to develop these talents into strengths, and how those strengths can be used in day to day interactions to complete school assignments, and determining possible career options. The best way to achieve this is to explore what your son likes to do and what his interests are.

Interest Identification

What is he interested in? What things does he do well? Your son's natural interests will be a better reference for helping him to determine what types of career paths he could one day pursue. Your job as his mentor will be to help your son determine how best to use his talents in daily interactions or to make the most of those things he is interested in. Some things will come more naturally, but once you've helped him identify his talents, a good next step is to identify his interests. To help you through the process, I've included an Interest Identification Worksheet. Through a series of questions, your son will be challenged to identify what he thinks his skills and interests are. Remember, his interests should manifest as specific activities or skills he can use to sharpen his talents.

Options for His Future

What do you want to be when you grow up? While I think this question is a little clichéd, it is still critically important for your son to begin thinking about his future—even as early as the age of 12. After the 'Great Recession' of 2008, my thought process about higher education and careers changed. I still believe that going to college and getting advanced degrees is the best way to sustained financial success; however, you cannot approach your college career in a wait and see manner. It is far too expensive (whether you pay for it as you go or once you are finished in the form of student loans) to approach college without a clear plan. A list of Career Alternatives is listed in Figure 5. It is not a comprehensive list, but offers a good cross section of the types of careers that can be considered. Additionally, when he starts to think about what he'd like to do "when he grows up" you can help him keep in mind what his talents and interests are in order to hone in on a specific career path.

As it relates to career selection and natural talents; you can make any career work well, as long as you are using your natural abilities. While there is no direct correlation between talents and careers; you should keep in mind that certain careers may be better suited for individuals that possess specific talents. For example, a child with Talent Descriptor of "Curious" could pursue roles as a physician, scientist, teacher, attorney, engineer, sales person, etc. However if he is not an incredibly outgoing person a young man with this talent, may not be best suited for a career in Sales or Entertainment. With all of that said, the primary driver should be what types of things he is interested in. This will drive his passion and keep him engaged over time.

You will notice that 'Entrepreneur' is not represented in the Career Alternatives chart. This is primarily because an individual can become an Entrepreneur through any or all of the paths listed. My point for introducing this into the conversation about *Options for His Future*, is to make sure that you talk about the benefits of 'being your own boss,' with your son. As referenced earlier about my thoughts after the 2008 economic meltdown—another reality for me that came out of it was that you have to maintain some control of your destiny. In my opinion, owning your own business or having a skill you can perform with your hands, like carpentry work, are important if you want to have more control over your own destiny. I am not necessarily advocating vocational programs over 'traditional' college, however for some boys it should be an option. My goal with the statement is to recommend that you keep that in mind as you guide your son about his future educational and career alternatives.

Your son can easily pick up a new skill, or at least the desire to learn more about a particular skill, when he completes projects throughout his young life. This will be especially true if he approaches his projects with the attitude that he could be learning a skill that could help him for the rest of his life.

Interest Identification Worksheet
Talents:
Skills/Interests:
What Do You Do Best, Naturally?
What Types of Activities Are You Drawn To?
What Skills/Knowledge Do You Pick Up Quickly?
What Types of Challenges Give you The Most Satisfaction?
Have You Ever Been Engrossed in What You Were Doing? Explain
What Type of Careers Interest You?

Figure 4: Interest Identification Worksheet

Broad Range of Industry Types				
Education	Research	Technology	Scientist	Law Enforcement
Law	Accounting	Aviation	Commun-ication	Firefighter
Healthcare	Music	Art	Construction	Carpenter
Engineering	Entertain-ment	Social Services	Public Service	Hospitality
Sales	Business	Farming	Sports	Health/Fit-ness

Figure 5: Career Alternatives

....

Nurturing your son's strengths is not just an exercise or a course. This role should be viewed as an ongoing, living, and growing part of his life. A theme that seemed to be commonplace among the men within my circle was that they unknowingly spent a large part of their youth and young adult life doing things that played to their strengths. The point is to identify his natural talent and cultivate the talent through skills and knowledge. As detailed in this chapter, when cultivated, your son's talents will be strengthened to the point that he can use them to perform at his best in day-to day interactions as well as the career field he chooses. While it is not necessary to go through a formal process to assess your son's talents, if after you've reviewed the material and would like to have your son assessed, go to www.1021leadership.org, for more information.

Chapter 11

Create a Vision and Success Plan
for the Future

Highlights	
"If you don't like the idea of following just any road, you need to take the steps to determine where you are going and how you will get there."	
− Develop a Vision Statement − Sample Vision Statement Worksheet − Priority Planning	− Sample Priority Planning Worksheet − Pulling It All Together − Success Plan Case Study

When you develop and follow a plan for success you have a much better chance of building a strong future and leaving a lasting legacy. In the previous chapter, I went through some of the steps the two of you can take to identify your son's talents, his interests and potential career options. In this chapter, the focus will be on the actual Success Planning process. Critical to this process is the creation of a vision statement that incorporates the learning's from Chapter 10. Additionally your son should go through the process of developing a timeline for achieving the vision and identify the specific milestones needed to do so. *While I think the process is simple, I don't recommend that you ask your son to go through this exercise unless he is mature enough to complete the worksheets with limited assistance.* Therefore when the time is right, I've included information about developing a Vision Statement and how to go about identifying the Priorities that are critical to achieving the vision. Also included in this chapter are Worksheets for each step to help make the process of defining the vision and timelines easier.

Develop a Vision Statement

A vision statement is a declaration that communicates the role an individual envisions playing in life, identifying the talents and abilities he will build and leverage to achieve the vision, along with the specific action steps needed to get him there. While it seems lofty, creating a vision is similar to setting goals; the key difference is the length of time that is devoted to the specific action steps— a vision is longer term, where goals are more short-term.

My advice is, "don't over-complicate what is needed to develop the vision statement." Your Vision Statement should include **What** you want to achieve and **How** you will achieve it. As you go through this exercise, keep in mind that your son's natural talents and interests will factor into the How. The statement should also, answer three primary questions:

a)   What is the end goal or the long-term vision?

b)   What big goals or milestones do you want to achieve on the path to becoming that?

c)   What actions will you take to achieve the goals?

Work with your son to complete the Vision Statement Worksheet in Figure 6. Once he has developed his statement, you should consider developing a family vision statement as well as your own individual vision statement, if you haven't already done so.

Priority Planning

To develop a success plan, you need to think through the steps you will take to accomplish your goals. Establishing a timeline or priority plan will help keep your son's long-term goals on track and will prove invaluable to his ability to actually achieve the goals he sets for himself. Have your son complete the Priority Planning Worksheet, in Figure 7. It will help him identify his most important goals and the specific action steps to achieve his vision. Overall, the Priority Planning is designed to help your son determine:

a)   What is most important to him?

b)   What can he achieve today toward that goal, based on his current abilities?

c)   What priorities link to the bigger vision or are most relevant today?

Remember priority planning is an evolutionary process.   For example, if a part of your son's vision is to one day attend college; because he is only 13 years old, it is probably not realisitc to make the actual admissions process a priority. What is more realistic is to possibly create a Community Service project that he can manage over the next couple of years. It certainly will be impressive to include the details of this type of initiative on his application for college in a few years. However he should probably wait until he is a bit older to include admissions-type activities, like completing the application or requesting letters of recommendation. As he gets older and revisits the Success Plan, he can update his priorities as appropriate.

Vision Statement Worksheet
What is Important to You (Define What You Are About):
What Big Goals Do You Want to Accomplish:
How Do You Expect to Accomplish Your Goals:
Use the Space Below to Draft Your Vision Statement:
Final Vision Statement:

Figure 6: Vision Statement Worksheet

Priority Planner				
Vision:				
Big Goals:		**Achieve By:**		
0 to 3 mos	3 to 6 mos	6 to 12 most	1 to 5 yrs	5 to 10 yrs

Figure 7: Priority Planner

Pulling it All Together

When you take the next step to develop a comprehensive Success Plan, your son effectively arms himself with the framework for establishing priorities and making better decisions. In *Pulling it All Together*, your son will take the information he gathered about his talents and interests in Chapter 10, along with his Vision Statement and Priority Plan, to create his actual Success Plan. At this point, no additional self-examination is required. Your son is simply pulling together everything he's uncovered to this point in one easily accessible document, that he can use to remind him of his vision. An actual Case Study of a completed Success Plan is included on upcoming pages to demonstrate what one can look like. Remember a plan can take on different forms; it just depends on how creative your son wants to be with it. The Case Study example is a straightforward document, but individuals also create posters with a combination of pictures and words that depict their goals and desires. Let your son determine what works best for him.

Once he has decided how to capture the details of his Success Plan, whether in a chart, like the Case Study example or a more elaborate poster; he should always keep it in plain view. As he achieves new goals shade them in. If he needs to move goals around to a different time period, do so, but don't remove them entirely. I think this will help manage progress and help you both understand why goals were or were not achieved.

Also keep in mind that once your son has created his Success Plan it is not set in stone. Things change, plans change and as your son grows and matures he will refine what is important to him. Therefore just as successful people and companies do—revisit the plan every now and again to adjust priorities and interests. Each time he does this, you both will discover something about him that you didn't know before.

Case Study: JM1 – is a young man I worked with during one of the pilot programs for the 10.2.1 Project. JM1 is 14 years old. He and his 10-year-old sister are being raised by their mother. James does have a reasonably good relationship with his father (sees him about twice per month). His family would be classified as middle income. He doesn't make the best grades, but this has more to do with focus. He is a natural leader and very good athlete. However, he has very lofty goals but doesn't necessarily possess the discipline right now to take the steps to achieve them. With his mother's help, he went through the first five questions on the Success Plan Worksheet. I helped him develop the final plan, including the vision statement and priority plan worksheet. His mother has committed to developing a plan for the entire family, herself and James' sister, using the same steps.

Name: ████████
Original Date: January 2011   **Rev Date:**
Talents: Charismatic, Assured, Curious
Skills/Interests: 1. Likes to meet new people and have fun 2. Football, Basketball and Track 3. Good at Math 4. Likes to be involved with teen church 5. Fearless and very Competitive
Big Goals: 1. Improve my final Grades (Math-A, Language Arts-B, Science-B) 2. Play on Varisity football team as a Freshman 3. Get a Division 1 football scholarship 4. Have the fastest 100 meter time in the state, for my age
Purpose: 1. Be a man of integrity and a good example for everyone around me
Vision Statement – Developed Based on above information
JM1 Vision Statement – I want to have the courage to make decisions that are in my best interest. Knowing who I am and what I want in life will ultimately allow me to reach my full potential. I want to grow in a way that is pleasing to God. I want to use my God-given talents to become succesful in the sports world, as either a professional football athlete or a sports agent. I want to have the confidence to use the power I have in me to make the changes that will help me achieve my long-term goals.

Case Study: JM1a

Timeline:				
0 to 3 mos	**3 to 6 mos**	**6 to 12 mos**	**1 to 5 yrs**	**5 to 10 yrs**
1-Turn in every homework assignment	1- Continue 1, 3, 4, 5 from previous 3 months	1- Continue 1, 3, 4, 5 from previous 3 months	1 - Contribute to Varsity Program as a Freshman	1 - Graduate with Bachelors degree early (within 3 years)
2- Request extra-credit work. Turn in work within 2 days of receipt	2 - Achieve a final grade of all B's or better in my core academic courses, and A's in all other courses (Honor Roll)	2-Begin school with better attitude and stronger work ethic		
3-Read 30 minutes every night	3-In first track meet, run sub 13 seconds in 100 yard dash	3 – Achieve all A's for every marking period.	2 - Graduate from High School as an Academic All-American	2 – Become drafted as a professional football player
4 - Complete all chores around the house when asked	4- attend 2 to 3 football camps	4–Have a record-breaking year in football		
5 - Run for 1 hour per day	5 - Qualify for the Junior Olympics in both 100 and 200 yard dash		3 - Receive a football scholarship	Plan B – Graduate from Law School

Case Study: JM1b

....

Planning is a process of introspection and breaking things down so that you can build exactly what you want. Very similar to how businesses create strategic plans; a Success Plan will get your son on track and keep him on track toward achieving his highest goals. Remember going through the process of developing a Success Plan should be one of the most fun and rewarding activities the two of you will do and will serve him well for the rest of his life.

Chapter 12

Make the Plan for Success Happen

Highlights		
"Certain personality characteristics can completely change the game and give you the ability to achieve success in a dramatic way."		
– Be Ready	– Live Relentlessly	– Have Resilience

Up to this point, the focus has been on taking an 'inside out' approach to developing your son, by helping him establish healthy relationships, building character, and having a definitive vision supported by a plan for success. This chapter, identifies the behavior—attitude—mindset—mentality...your son must possess to make the plan actually happen. From my observation and experience, I absolutely, without doubt, believe that the combination of being—READY, RELENTLESS and RESILIENT describes the mentatlity that is required to completely 'change the game' and drive your son's success in a dramatic way.

Characteristic	Description
Ready	When you have proactively prepared yourself for the kinds of opportunities that are in alignment with your vision—you are READY! When you anticipate the challenges that may occur along the way and are mentally prepared to combat them—you are READY! When you engage in a habitual system of preparation that enables you to manage your life more effectively—you are READY!
Relentless	When you are in aggressive pursuit of the short and long-term goals that link to your plan for success—you are RELENTLESS! When you refuse to let obstacles or barriers get in your way—you are RELENTLESS! When you are completely engaged and focused on the end result and have an 'at-all-cost,' attitude about getting there—you are RELENTLESS!
Resilient	When you possess a positive attitude about your abilities and consistently recover from disappointments, setbacks and obstacles—you are RESILIENT! When you possess the flexibility of mind and attitude to make adjustments when the original plan falls apart—you are RESILIENT! When you are fueled by overcoming obstacles and become more determined to achieve in the face of setbacks—you are RESILIENT!

Figure 8: Ready, Relentless and Resilient Defined

At one time or another we all hopefully demonstrate these characteristics. The reason why we don't all achieve wild success is because we don't demonstrate them at the same time and certainly not on a consistent basis. Achieving this mentality is an evolutionary process and will take time to become second nature to your son. Throughout this book, I have presented you with many opportunities to help your son develop these traits, whether it is through the process of building positive relationships, working through a project or using a systematic approach to decision making, your son will have a chance to increase his level of readiness, relentlessness and resilience. In Figure 8, I provided examples of what the behavior of each of these characteristics look like. In the upcoming sections, I will share specific strategies that you can focus on with your son to nurture this mentality. Some of them may seem to overlap but that further demonstrates how inter-connected these characteristics are. With that said, as you work with him to build these crtitical traits; remember, it will take consistent effort over time, so that they become part of his DNA.

Be Ready

If your son wants to achieve his plan for success he must be prepared for every situation or opportunity that comes his way. The following strategies will help you get your son in the habit of proactively approaching all aspects of his life:

Be Prepared for Each Day – As your son gets older, probably around 4th or 5th grade, his teachers may require that he keep a daily planner. I suggest you get him started before it is a requirement, so he will be in the habit of preparing for each day. The value of this exercise is not so much in the physical act of noting activities. The value comes from him thinking about what is on his plate and mentally preparing himself to meet the demands each day will require. Aside from the obvious organizational benefits, it also establishes a way of thinking and helps him to place value on his time. My advice would be to start simple by letting him see you maintain one for the family. When you think he's ready, purchase an age appropriate planner to get him in the mindset of maintaining it.

Anticipate and Be Prepared for Events – Just as with the goal of being prepared for each day, the process of mentally anticipating major events and being ready to take them on as a challenge is about preparation. These are not necessarily the types of events that will be documented in his Success Plan; they represent bigger day-to-day activities. For example, if your son has a big presentation in class, he has to approach it just as he would any project, but most important is that he be mentally prepared prior to the event. The biggest difference between this type of event and day-to-day activities is the amount of effort that will ultimately be required to complete the task. He can use the planner to prepare himself, but what it helps to reinforce is that he must be mentally proactive about his life.

Live Relentlessly

No matter what he does in life, your son can benefit from an attitude that, "he is playing to win." You just need to qualify for him, what 'winning' means. Winning is not as black and white as win or lose, it is about the process of your son preparing, pursuing and getting himself mentally ready to deliver his best effort. When he actually shows up for the event or activity, it is simply a performance. The goal is to help your son appreciate the process of preparation and giving his full effort more than the win itself. As you know, we live in a very competitive society; and most individuals, his friends included, will not view 'winning' in these terms. Because of that, it will require that you are constantly in your son's ear about the significance of the process and not the performance that takes place on the day of the event. *The easiest way to get this message across is by helping him identify a sport, event, or activity he can get motivated or passionate about and get him involved. Doing so should also inspire his natural competitiveness and desire to win. Use the following strategies to stimulate a relentless mentality in your son:*

Identify His Passion – It will be easier to get your son motivated about the process of preparation and full effort when he is passionate about the activity. When you identify his strengths and coach him through the success planning process he will be able to identify several things he likes to do. When he does nail down a few things, I would recommend that you focus on getting him involved in them or activities that are closely related. If you haven't gone through the process of developing a Success Plan or you think he is still too young to go through the process, a shortcut is to simply think about the things that maintain his interest for long periods of time? Another way to look at this is to determine what is the thing or activity you think he does extremely well. Once these activities have been identified, you now have a sense of the types of activities that he should engage in to help cultivate that relentless mentality.

Inspire Competition – Competition, if kept in perspective can be extremely positive and fun. It also serves as the training ground for building a relentless mentality. When your son is placed in competitive situations he learns to operate in a state of opposing wills. Competition can come in the form of individual activities (for example, rock climbing) or team sports. For some children, being part of a team can become boring over time. To keep his interest in the team, I recommend that you encourage your son to develop his own goals within the competition. For example if he plays on a soccer team; the team's goal is to win. However his goal could be to become more aggressive about "driving to the goal and making attempts to score." Doing this will make the experience/activity more relevant and engaging for him. As he gets older, he won't require this to stay engaged with the team, but as a way to set stretch goals for himself. Ultimately gaining experience in competitive situations will give your son the stamina to push through adversarial situations and leave him with a 'stick-with-it' mentality. So look for opportunities to get him involved in competitive situations as much as possible.

Have Resilience

Resilience is a deep inner strength. It gets stronger with each situation that requires you to get back on your horse after you fall. As a single mother, you probably already know how critical this mentality is, because you may do it everyday. However your son may not find it so easy and will require a little help. I can honestly say that resilience was not an innate quality for me. Thankfully, I have acquired it over the years by pushing through obstacles and recovering from disappointing situations. You can build resilience in your son, starting early and as he matures his ability to recover when faced with setbacks will improve. If your son's ability to be resilient is slow to emerge, consider the following:

Don't Let Him Quit – As his mother, you have to make sure, no matter how tempting, you never allow your son to quit. Children have a tendency to want to quit, when they become bored or don't feel they are good at an activity or believe the going is too tough. This is certainly not unique to single mothers, but I notice that mothers with the best of intentions will sometimes give in to the whining and complaining when a child wants to quit. In some instances you may feel as if you are protecting your son or preserving his confidence in some way. Well, if he makes a habit of quitting it will be much easier for him to give up when the situation is more critical. If he encounters a situation that is really troubling or difficult for him, be prepared to coach him through it and only intervene if needed. For example, if he is performing in a play and has a personality conflict with the director; talk to him about the value of sticking with the commitment and give him strategies for dealing with this uncomfortable situation (or person in this example). When it is time to sign-up for the next play he has the option of trying it again or moving on to do something else.

More complex situations like the one just described will happen when he is older, but until then we can start cultivating the mentality of resilience much, much earlier. For instance, a toddler learning how to walk will fall down many times before he finally gets his stride. Throughout your son's young life, he will learn to master many developmental milestones. The important thing to remember is that they won't all go smoothly. Just like you did when he was learning to walk, when he falls you must insist that he get back up—quickly, and try it again. But before he tries it again encourage him to figure out what the problem is and determine what adjustment he should make to have a better outcome. When you consistently encourage this process of conquering problems, over time he will develop the innate strength needed to overcome obstacles and will be able to work through pain, boredom as well as negative feelings and will not think twice about giving up.

Be Flexible and Explore Different Options – Help your son develop a flexible attitude toward completing projects. Resilient men find it easy to bounce back because they aren't as tied to doing things in a specific way. If your son learns to step out-of-the box and choose a different approach, path, or option to achieving his goals, he will become more comfortable with alternative ways of doing things. When he is faced with inevitable disappointments or setback he won't let them get him down, as he will have already done the work to determine another way to approach it.

....

Whether they employ all of these characteristics at once or as they need them, without them it is virtually impossible to achieve success in a significant or sustained way. Chapter 12 may have been one of the shortest chapters, but it certainly is the most significant, because none of the information you received or the plans created to help your son, mean much, if they are never acted on. Now that you have the strategies to help your son form the mentality he will need to make his plan happen—take the next step and motivate him to success—be his Champion!

Conclusion

I am passionate about finding ways to support and encourage the growth and development of young men, especially those facing less than ideal circumstances. I don't profess to be an expert, but I have presented one approach that focuses on 4 critical priorities, complete with numerous strategies and ideas you can use to help position your son to achieve unparalleled personal and professional success. I decided on these priorities using key aspects of my own journey that proved most helpful as I evolved from one of three boys raised by a single mother in the inner city to an key management role on Wall Street. I hope you were able to determine how you will incorporate these priorities into the fabric of you and your son's life:

1)   *Establish a healthy relationship with your son and support his need to establish and maintain relationships with others including his father.*

2)   *Stress the importance of 'self' mastery with your son, starting with self-discipline, and combining it with a healthy level of self-respect and the ability to make good decisions, every time.*

3)   *Maximize every opportunity available to support your effort to raise a successful son. For example, the educational system, tried and true financial concepts, mentors, role models and numerous resources you can tap, as early as today.*

4)   *Define a clear path to success by identifying his natural talents, taking the steps to help him develop a plan for success, and sharing, with him, the keys to making it all happen. Which are being ready to seize an opportunity, relentless about pursuing and achieving his goals, and resilient in the face of adversity and uncertainty.*

As discussed in this book, helping your son along this journey will take a concerted effort from you. I know all single mothers aren't living off of adrenaline, going from one stress to the next; however some are and I can imagine that this stress compounded with the thought of spending even more time in parenting mode may seem daunting. If you haven't already implemented some of these strategies in your parenting, doing so will require a little extra time initially. But, after a while streamlining your approach to parenting should ultimately save you time and yield better results. Until you get to that point, I've provided a few more strategies that are just for you. They are intended to help you manage the rigors of all you do.

Prepare Yourself for the Journey Ahead

As a busy parent myself, I can now fully appreciate how difficult it was for my mother to get from one day to the next. As a matter of fact, at times the stress in my adult life very closely resembles the life I remember growing up. I think the key difference now is that I understand the importance of taking a more proactive approach to managing the stress from day to day—and it all boils down to taking it one day at a time.

In order to accomplish this, I would suggest that you break up your day into sections: 1) when you wake, take time to <u>connect</u>, 2) the active part of the day is time to <u>execute</u> your plan, 3) In the evening hours, take a few minutes to develop a <u>plan</u> that will help you manage the following day, 4) as you close out your evening, take time to <u>re-connect</u> and give thanks for the many blessings and lessons you received on that day. Breaking down your day in this way helps to provide structure to your own mental space and will lead to a better night's sleep and more production on the following day.

Connect: Take the First 10 Minutes for Faith – Starting your day in a peaceful state is a great way to minimize stress. Take the first 10 minutes of your day to meditate and open the spiritual connection to your source. This may appear to be a small portion of your day, but these 10 minutes have the potential to make a major impact and set the tone for your entire day.

Execute: Make Progress Daily – Making tangible progress toward a goal each and every day will help you get mentally organized and goes a long way toward minimizing stress. Having a daily plan in place that outlines your daily tasks, which could include work and home, is an important second step. Many of us operate without a plan and do okay. However with a plan you can prioritize tasks and give the appropriate amount of attention to them. Even if you are already good about writing down a daily plan, consistently making progress on that plan seems to be a much more difficult thing to master for most of us. There are no quick fixes for helping you make progress toward your daily plan. It boils down to discipline and forming new habits if you need them.

Plan: Prepare for a Successful Day – Planning your day is a good way of organizing your mental space. Most of us understand the importance of keeping your home organized and free of as much clutter as possible. It helps you think. This same principle applies to organizing your day as it will prepare you to make the most of your time. *Most mothers are probably already using day planners or journals in the workplace. So it should be easy to incorporate into your journal the more important family tasks that are on your plate. Remember, with all the new projects your son will be undertaking, you'll have to keep him on top of a few more things.*

Re-connect: Share Your Blessings and Lessons – If you are reading this book, congratulations, you have at least 5 things to be thankful for. We often think that things aren't worthy of mentioning unless it is a 'big deal.' It is often the small things that make the biggest impact in our lives. Get a journal or planner to place beside your bed and jot down at least 5 things you were thankful for that day. It could be the same journal you use to plan your day. But get in the habit of doing it every day.

....

The future begins now. And you are more prepared than ever – so is your son.

Sources

1. Heather Sipsma, Teenage fathers often born to teenage fathers. In: Yale School of Public Health study. http://opa.yale.edu. Published January 14, 2010, Accessed April 25, 2011

2. G.D. Sandefur (et al.), "The Effects of Parental Marital Status…," Social Forces, September 1992

3. http://www.divorcerate.org/

4. Maureen Downey. New national dropout rates: 25 percent of all students; nearly 40 percent of black and Hispanic kids fail to graduate on time, The Atlanta Journal-Constitution Web site, http://blogs.ajc.com/get-schooled-blog/2010/06/02/new-national-dropout-rates-25-percent-of-all-students-nearly-40-percent-of-black-and-hispanic-kids-fail-to-graduate-on-time. Published June 2, 2010, Accessed April 25, 2011

5. J.B. Stedman (et.al.), "Dropping Out," Congressional Research Service Report No. 88-417, 1988

6. Alan Beck; US Bureau of Justice Statistics, Survey of State Prison Inmates 1991, Survey of Youth in Custody, 1987, US Bureau of Justice Statistics, 1988

7. Alan Beck et al., US Bureau of Justice Statistics, Survey of State Prison Inmates 1991 Survey of Youth in Custody, 1987, US Bureau of Justice Statistics, 1988

8. Zill and Nord, "Running in Place," Child Trends. 1994

9. Vaden-Kiernan N, Ialongo N, Pearson J, Kellam S. Household family structure and children's aggressive behavior: A longitudinal study of urban elementary school children. *Journal of Abnormal Child Psychology,* 1995; 23 (5):553-558. http://www.springerlink.com/content/0091-0627/?k=household+family+structure. Accessed April 25, 2011

10. Alan Beck (et al.), Survey of Youth in Custody, 1987, US Bureau of Justice Statistics, 1988, Source

11. J.L. Sheline (et al.), "Risk Factors…,"American Journal of Public Health, No. 84. 1994 Source

12. U.S. Dept. of Health and Human Services, Survey on Child Health (1993) Ralph McNeal, Sociology of Education 88. 1995

13. And N. Davidson, "Life without Father," Policy Review. 1990, Source: D. Cornell (et al.), Behavioral Sciences and the Law, 5. 1987

14. L.M.C. Bisnairs (ET at.), American Journal of Orthopsychiatry, no 60 (1990)

15. U.S. Department of Education, National Center for Education Statistics, Statistics of Public Elementary and Secondary Day Schools,1955–56 through 1984–85; Common Core of Data (CCD), "State Nonfiscal Survey of Public Elementary/Secondary Education," 1985–86 through 2007–08, and National Elementary and Secondary Enrollment Model, 1972–2007

16. National Center for Higher Education Management Systems, "Racial/Ethnic Gaps: Percent of Adults with an Associate Degree or Higher-Gaps between Whites and Minorities" (Boulder: NCHEMS, 2009).

17. Marcus Buckingham, Donald Clifton, "Now, Discover Your Strengths, 2001; All rights reserved. Gallup®, Gallup Consulting®, Clifton StrengthsFinder® are trademarks of Gallup, Inc.

About The Author

Throughout his career, Zachary Hawkins has directed and managed a number of successful domestic and international strategic initiatives, and possesses over 20 years of sales and marketing experience across the financial services, pharmaceutical and telecommunications industries. Through much of his career, he has remained engaged in the community, serving on the YMCA's Sustaining Committee to preserve youth programs, and occupying both formal and informal mentoring roles to help colleagues and youth organizations with their professional development.

As a member of Alpha Phi Alpha Fraternity, Inc., Hawkins has worked with *Big Brothers Big Sisters of America* to mentor and inspire young people to achieve new and greater heights. Recently, he was named "Certified Strengths Advocate" by the Clifton School, a Gallup organization that specializes in strengths-based career development and education.

Recently, Hawkins launched *10 to 1 Leadership*, a leadership mentoring organization geared towards helping young boys and men set and accomplish concrete goals that will guide them towards meaningful academic and career success.

Hawkins lives in New Jersey with his wife, Karen, and sons, ZJ and Zion. He also has a daughter, Jazmine, who resides in Texas.

www.ingramcontent.com/pod-product-compliance
Lightning Source LLC
Chambersburg PA
CBHW021333090426
42742CB00008B/588